TRUST
IN EVERY
MOMENT

TRUST
IN EVERY
MOMENT

A Journey Toward God

Susan N. Perelka

REDEMPTION PRESS

© 2023 by Susan N. Perelka. All rights reserved.

Published by Redemption Press, PO Box 427, Enumclaw, WA 98022, (360) 226-3488.

Redemption Press is honored to present this title in partnership with the author. The views expressed or implied in this work are those of the author. Redemption Press provides our imprint seal representing design excellence, creative content, and high-quality production.

Noncommercial interests may reproduce portions of this book without the express written permission of the author, provided the text does not exceed five hundred words. When reproducing text from this book, include the following credit line: "*Trust in Every Moment: A Journey toward God* by Susan N. Perelka. Used by permission."

Commercial interests: No part of this publication may be reproduced in any form, stored in a retrieval system, or transmitted in any form by any means—electronic, photocopy, recording, or otherwise—without prior written permission of the publisher/author, except as provided by United States of America copyright law.

Unless otherwise indicated, all Scripture quotations are from the *ESV® Bible (The Holy Bible,* English *Standard Version®),* Copyright © 2001 by Crossway, a publishing ministry of Good News Publishers. Used by permission. All rights reserved.

Scripture quotations marked (NIV) are taken from the Holy Bible, New International Version®, NIV®. Copyright © 1973, 1978, 1984, 2011 by Biblica, Inc.™ Used by permission of Zondervan. All rights reserved worldwide. www.zondervan.com The "NIV" and "New International Version" are trademarks registered in the United States Patent and Trademark Office by Biblica, Inc.™

Scripture quotations marked (MSG) are taken from THE MESSAGE, copyright © 1993, 2002, 2018 by Eugene H. Peterson. Used by permission of NavPress. All rights reserved. Represented by Tyndale House Publishers, a Division of Tyndale House Ministries.

ISBN 13: 978-1-951350-44-4 (Paperback)
978-1-951350-45-1 (eBook)

Library of Congress Catalog Card Number: 2024907943

*In loving memory of my dear friend,
Kathleen Anne Linger.
Your life has been an example of trust
in our sovereign God.
May we follow your example and
trust God no matter what.*

CONTENTS

Acknowledgments.. ix

1. Trust in Adversity 1
    But Why?... 3
    Just a Matter of Time 5
    Tried but Not Forsaken 9
    I Know until I Don't 13
    Whom Do You Belong To? 17
2. Trust in Unknown Circumstances 21
    Unknown Destination 23
    Unknown Sacrifice 27
    Unknown Timing 31
    Unknown Plan 35
3. Trust in Known Circumstances 41
    Known for a Purpose 43
    Known with a Risk 47
    Known to Move Forward 51
    Known yet Confident 55
4. Trust in Unfair Circumstances 59
    Unfair and Did Nothing 61
    Unfair and Falsely Accused 65
    Unfair and Forgotten 69
    Unfair yet Good 73
5. Trust in the Impossible 77
    Humbly Accepting the Impossible 79
    Comparing the Impossible 83
    Moving Forward in the Impossible 87
    Eyes on the Impossible 91

6. Trust When You Are Called 95
   Called with Proof 97
   Called with Assurance 101
   Called to Plant Seeds 105
   Called to Life Eternal 109
   Called to Save 113

7. Trust When You Don't Understand 117
   What Is an Ark? 119
   What's the Plan? 123
   Why Are You Cast Down? 127
   How Can This Be Good? 131

8. What Trust Does for You 135
   An Undivided Heart 137
   Courage under Fire 141
   A Life of Rejoicing 145
   Joy in Obedience 149
   A Testimony of Praise 153

9. Why God Is Worthy of Our Trust 157
   Guidance from the Sovereign Planner 159
   Protection from the Creator 163
   Certainty in His Trustworthiness 167
   Confident In the Goodness of God 171
   He Is God and We Are Not 175

ACKNOWLEDGMENTS

I cannot begin to thank my loved ones and friends without first thanking my heavenly Father. In His sovereign plan, He has brought me along this journey of lessons, people, and situations, causing me to learn so many aspects of trusting Him no matter what.

My love for my family is deep, and I am so thankful for what I have learned through them and the support they have given me as I started this new journey of writing. Thanks to my husband, Greg, for believing in me and encouraging me along the way, and to my children, Bryan, Branden, Benjamin, and Bethany. You are my heart.

Stephanie Dalton, Carrie Puff, Tonya Harwood, and Chelsey Martin, you are my greatest cheerleaders! Thank you for your excitement from the start, your faith in me through this project, and for just being there. I love all of you so much.

I cannot end without thanking my pastors, Mark Ashley and Eric Puff. I love assisting you both in ministry. You have blessed me by challenging me to think, teaching me truth, and walking alongside me as I have learned more each day what it means to trust God.

INTRODUCTION

Trust is defined in the dictionary[1] as a "firm belief in the reliability, truth, ability, or strength of someone or something." But how firm is my trust when I quickly lose faith during confusing times, when I cannot see the way? I struggle to have hope when difficulties pile on top of one another and the challenges have no end. I lose confidence when I cannot fix the wrongs or make situations around me better. Life brings hard seasons, sometimes all at once. I feel like I am lost and alone, without faith and in despair, unsure of whom or what to trust, where to turn, or how to move forward. Times like this cause me to look for strength, reliability, and something to place my trust in … or someone.

Alone in the struggle to trust? No. The Word of God shares story after story of the faith journeys of God's people. While the hardships and difficulties during Bible times differ from today, Abraham, Job, Joseph, Esther, and others agonized over unfair, unknown, adverse circumstances. They had times of feeling lost and without hope, but each found God faithful. Their stories are recorded to assure us that God alone is worthy of our trust. Even in our lifetime, examples in the lives of believers of trust in our sovereign God bring encouragement as we move forward in our own walk of faith.

---

1 Oxford Languages, s.v. "Trust," accessed November 15, 2023, 2024 Oxford University Press, https://www.oed.com/search/dictionary/?scope=Entries&q=trust.

Our life is a continuous journey of learning to trust Him. Every difficulty crossing our path gives us a choice of where we will place our trust. Every choice to trust God deepens our level of faith in Him. Can we trust God's faithfulness to carry us through whatever comes along our journey? How can we know we can trust Him in every moment? It starts as we take a step of faith toward God.

*Blessed is the man who trusts in the Lord,
whose trust is the Lord.*

JEREMIAH 17:7

TRUST IN ADVERSITY

Why, Lord? Why the difficulties? When will the troubles stop? Is this Your way of getting my attention, or is it so others see You? I can't see You. All I can see is what is going on around me, but You have promised You are here. Even in difficult times, I can trust You in every moment.

BUT WHY?

But I trust in you, O Lord; I say, "You are my God."

PSALM 31:14

News stories recount the horrors of war, violence, kidnappings.

Hurricanes blast disastrous winds that destroy.

Forest fires blacken acres of land, leading to the loss of property, animals, and people.

I sit by the bedside of my critically ill friend, who is battling cancer and knows life is losing its hold.

I hug a friend close as she mourns the loss of her precious child.

So much hardship and sadness can overwhelm us. Sometimes I wonder where the good is. Is God good? Of course! I know with certainty that God is good. We have a good God, but why, then? Why would a good God let His children go through the hard times?

In Psalm 31, David's description of his life includes affliction, distress, sorrow, and grief. Some of the sorrow he bears is the result of his sins, yet some is caused by his enemies. He describes himself as being a reproach or dread to his neighbors and acquaintances. Those same descriptions can be used to describe the hardship and sadness we face.

As David opens the psalm, he right away claims God as his refuge and then proceeds to work through what he is facing. Despite all this difficulty, David confidently says, "But I trust in you, O Lord; I say, 'You are my God.' My times are in your hand; rescue me from the hand of my enemies and from my persecutors! Make your face shine on your servant; save me in your steadfast love!" (Psalm 31:14–16).

So that gets back to my original question: Then why? Why the hardship, why the suffering and the evil? While some can result from our own sinful choices, most suffering is the result of sin in the world. Through our suffering, God makes His glory known. He is seen so clearly as He cares for His own. He shows Himself by giving us strength in our greatest times of need. He invites us to take Him as the refuge we so desperately need.

David claimed God as his refuge from the start. A place of safety is a place of trust, and his place of safety is God.

David ends this psalm by encouraging us to "be strong, and let your heart take courage, all you who wait for the Lord!" (v. 24).

God is not after making life easy for us. He is after our heart. The hard things in life cause us to seek Him and know Him more. The hard times help others see Him.

How have you seen God's goodness as you face the hard things? What keeps you from seeking your refuge in Him?

_____

_____

_____

In His goodness, God uses difficulties for our good, strengthening our trust in Him and for His glory, as others see Him.

JUST A MATTER OF TIME

For everything there is a season, and a time for every matter under heaven.

ECCLESIASTES 3:1

Time is a funny thing. We have all the time in the world; then suddenly we have no time. We need to fill our time, yet there never seems to be enough time. Our time is full, yet time also escapes. I think I have time to get one more thing done; then suddenly I am out of time. Where did the time go? It's so easy to lose track of our time.

Solomon writes in Ecclesiastes 3:1–2, "For everything there is a season, and a time for every matter under heaven: a time to be born, and a time to die; a time to plant, and a time to pluck up what is planted," and he continues. Time is in God's hands. He is the Creator of all things, including time—our time.

John Paton served as a Protestant missionary to the New Hebrides Islands of the South Pacific beginning in 1858. His greatest desire throughout his entire ministry was to share Jesus Christ and His saving grace with the natives. He suffered the loss of his wife and infant son and endured the animosity of the natives year after year, yet he continually showed them God's love. Many times he faced death, literally having a weapon raised right above him as a cannibal chief was ready to strike a blow, but he trusted the Lord. Paton explained, "As I had only once to die, I was content to leave the time and place and means in the hand of God."[2] He knew that unless God was ready to call him home, he was safe. It didn't matter what danger he appeared to be in; he was in God's hands. The situation was in God's control.

John Paton's time remained in God's hands. He knew as Paul did that "for to me to live is Christ, and to die is gain" (Philippians 1:21). "A time to be born and a time to die" (Ecclesiastes 3:2). A time to serve until God called him home. God's time for Paton to die was in 1907 after many dangerous but incredible years of ministry, resulting in the entire island of Aniwa professing Jesus Christ as their Lord and Savior. God enabled Paton to make good use of his earthly time, and he completely trusted in the work God gave him to do.

God has a purpose for the time He has given us. Whatever earthly time God provides for each of us, our purpose remains to glorify Him in all that we do with the use of the time He has given us.

What are you doing with what God allows to take place in your life?
What are you doing with your time?
How are you fulfilling God's purpose for you?

_____

_____

_____

---

2 John G. Paton, *The Story of John G. Paton: Or Thirty Years Among South Sea Cannibals* (n.p.: Adansonia Publishing, 1894). https://www.goodreads.com/author/quotes/207278.John_G_Paton.

___

___

___

*Make time to live for Christ, and trust Him for the work
He gives you to do.*

TRIED BUT NOT FORSAKEN

But he knows the way that I take; when he has tried me, I shall come out as gold.

JOB 23:10

I received a call one day from a woman who knew our church was a collection site for wheelchairs. She was seeking replacement footrests for the safety of her friend who had just suffered a stroke and easily fell forward without foot support to hold her in place. The woman continued to share the further suffering of this friend and others in an apartment complex, which had also just experienced flooding during the Christmas holiday as a result of frozen pipes bursting during the frigid temperatures. Many residents were elderly with disabilities and little money, and renter's insurance was not expected to cover the cost for many. While some had basic needs being cared for, the direness of the situation saddened my heart. These people were facing much adversity.

With no available footrests or funding to care for these people, there was little I could do except promise to pray. Yet this was the best thing I could do. I could not solve their problems, but I knew God could. Even if they felt God wasn't working in their situations, He was. God knew what each of these people needed and how to help them far more than I could. I know some would say how unfair this situation was for them or they did nothing to deserve it, but as we look at Job, we could say the same for him.

In his day, Job was a righteous, famous man. He enjoyed a large family and was blessed with land, an abundance of flocks, and servants. God pointed out the genuine uprightness of Job to Satan one day. Questioning Job's love for God, Satan credited it to the abundance of blessings rather than a genuine love and trust in God. So the challenge was issued by Satan. Soon Job lost everything in moments. He had done nothing to cause the calamities; he lived a life of genuine faith in his God. Job could not see God working, but he knew God was.

> Behold, I go forward, but he is not there, and backward, but I do not perceive him; on the left hand when he is working, I do not behold him; he turns to the right hand, but I do not see him. But he knows the way that I take; when he has tried me, I shall come out as gold. My foot has held fast to his steps; I have kept his way and have not turned aside. I have not departed from the commandment of his lips; I have treasured the words of his mouth more than my portion of food. (Job 23:8–12)

Job held fast to God because he knew the character of God. Though his circumstances had changed dramatically, he knew his God had not. He trusted the God he had trusted from the beginning though he could not understand His ways or see His work.

We may not see God at work, but He always is. Even when we feel alone or when things are especially hard, He is using the circumstances. He uses all things to bring His perfect plans together for our good and His glory.

Where does adversity in your life take you?
How does adversity cause you to see God differently?
In past adversity, what have you learned about God?

_____

_____

_____

_____

Trust an unchanging God through changing circumstances.

I KNOW UNTIL I DON'T

Great is our Lord, and abundant in power; his understanding is beyond measure.

PSALM 147:5

Traveling to China more than eight years ago, our family visited many provinces throughout the country. We enjoyed the beauty of the country and the culture, but I felt a bit lost in all our adventures. Many cultural things I had no understanding of but had the opportunity to learn. The language, however, I could not understand and would have needed much time and skill to learn. Though the dear Chinese people would try to communicate with me, I had no understanding. I did not know their language or their ways.

Sometimes I find the same in my walk with God. He is working through my life and in those around me, and I totally understand what is happening all around me. I know the next steps—until I don't. I feel like I have lost my way because I no longer see God's path. I have no understanding of what He is doing or how to move forward.

David seemed to accept this about God as he writes, "Great is our Lord, and abundant in power; his understanding is beyond measure" (Psalm 147:5). Our amazing God created an incredible universe in a week. He knew me and each person and what we would be like from the beginning of time. How could His understanding not be beyond measure? I could never begin to understand His plans, His ways. He has a perfect plan; clearly, He is capable of great things, more than I can even imagine.

At the end of the book of Job, this incredibly wise man realized the omnipotence of God:

> I know that you can do all things, and that no purpose of yours can be thwarted. "Who is this that hides counsel without knowledge?" Therefore I have uttered what I did not understand, things too wonderful for me, which I did not know. "Hear, and I will speak; I will question you, and you make it known to me." I had heard of you by the hearing of the ear, but now my eye sees you; therefore I despise myself, and repent in dust and ashes. (Job 42:2–6)

Job realized that all he knew or thought he knew about God and His ways, His greatness, was nothing close to who God is. He realized God was far above him. Job's suffering made sense to God, even though it didn't make sense to Job. God had not explained it or justified it to Job.

God alone knows His plan and what needs to take place for that plan to come to fruition. It is beyond man's understanding.

Job did not end up with a solution to his difficulties, but in seeing God as He is, his pressure was lightened as he drew closer to God. He knew he could trust God's plan.

We cannot always know God's ways or His plans. Sometimes He lets us know the path, but other times He knows it is better for us not to know. He invites us to trust Him, no matter what we see around us or what we think we understand. He invites us to trust Him because He understands far above what we ever could.

Are you lost in your understanding of your journey?
How has seeking an understanding affected your view of God?
What steps can you take when you don't understand?

_____

_____

_____

_____

*Trust your journey with the One whose understanding is
beyond measure.*

WHOM DO YOU BELONG TO?

Fear not, for I have redeemed you;
I have called you by name, you are mine.

ISAIAH 43:1

We all want to belong to someone or something. I belong to my family. I belong to my friends, to my church, to my city, country, and world. I am a part of or tied to something, which gives me a feeling of security or support because of the acceptance or identity of being a part of that group.

We all want to belong, but sometimes even as a part of these groups, I don't feel I belong. I feel lost and alone. I am journeying alone. I am looking for a place to belong.

Over and over in Scripture, God reminds us that He is with us. That we do belong—to Him. I love how Isaiah describes this:

> But now thus says the Lord, he who created you, O Jacob, he who formed you, O Israel: "Fear not, for I have redeemed you; I have called you by name, you are mine. When you pass through the waters, I will be with you; and through the rivers, they shall not overwhelm you; when you walk through fire you shall not be burned, and the flame shall not consume you. For I am the Lord your

God, the Holy One of Israel, your Savior."
(Isaiah 43:1–3)

Walking through the fire and not being burned reminded me of Shadrach, Meshach, and Abednego. Along with Daniel, they were taken captive by the Babylonians to serve in the king's palace and learn the Babylonian ways. They were the best of the best. Impressed, the king put Shadrach, Meshach, and Abednego in high positions, angering the Babylonian leaders. Convincing King Nebuchadnezzar to build a golden statue of himself, these men felt sure Shadrach, Meshach, and Abednego would not bow down to anyone other than their God, though the penalty was death in the fiery furnace.

As predicted, when the music sounded, the three Jewish men did not bow down. In fierce anger Nebuchadnezzar commanded the furnace to be heated seven times hotter. They were thrown into the fires, yet they were not afraid. Shadrach, Meshach, and Abednego knew, no matter what, they were going to be obedient to God. They belonged to Him. They trusted Him. They had no fear. And He was there. They were thrown into the fire, yet the flames did not touch them. Instead, King Nebuchadnezzar and the Babylonians' hearts were touched, and they turned in worship of the one true God.

That same God is with me. Even when the things I pass through seem incredibly hard and overwhelming, I can trust. I can have no fear. I belong to Him. He has called me by name, and I am His. He is always with me, and He is with each of you as well.

We don't always understand the fires He asks us to walk through, but we are assured so often that God is sovereign and in control of all things. We may not understand, but God is at work and doing a new thing. He will always make a way. "Remember not the former things, nor consider the things of old. Behold, I am doing a new thing; now it springs forth, do you not perceive it? I will make a way in the wilderness and rivers in the desert" (Isaiah 43:18–19).

Where do you belong?
How do your trials cause you to feel alone?
In what ways do you see God walking you through your fires?

_____

_____

_____

_____

Hold on to the hand of our Creator, who says,
"You are mine."

TRUST IN UNKNOWN CIRCUMSTANCES

Oh, Lord, I just have no idea what is going to happen here. Not knowing makes me feel so insecure and out of control. The waiting makes me anxious—if I could just know what's next or if all will be okay. But I can't know. You know though. Nothing is beyond Your knowledge, God, so I can be assured that even when I do not know everything, I can trust You in every moment.

UNKNOWN DESTINATION

Now the Lord said to Abram, "Go from your country and your kindred and your father's house to the land that I will show you." ... So Abram went, as the Lord had told him.

GENESIS 12:1, 4

Work, laundry, dinner, dishes, litter boxes, bill paying—never-ending tasks fill my daily, never-completed list. How I wish I could just get away! And I did! Away I went on a plane bound for Denver, Colorado, with my husband. I was offered a quiet hotel room with a peek at the distant mountains while he attended a conference.

While I have never spent much time on the western side of the United States, I knew my destination—the high plains of Denver surrounded by the foothills of the snowcapped Rocky Mountains. Most of us like to know the plan, the next steps. We would like to be in charge of our destination. This was not the case for Abram.

God called Abram to an unknown destination when He spoke to him. "Now the Lord said to Abram, 'Go from your country and your kindred and your father's house to the land that I will show you.' ... So Abram went, as the Lord had told him" (Genesis 12:1, 4). God simply told him to go to an unknown destination, and without question,

Abram packed up with his wife, Sarai, and left all they knew. The word *unknown* means there is nothing known or familiar within the span of one's knowledge, experience, or understanding. Abram moved forward with God, trusting He would do as He said and show him the land God had chosen for him.

I don't know about you, but going to a place I have not been but have knowledge of is different from simply leaving all I know to follow God to a place I have not heard of and know nothing of. That is where Abram's incredible trust comes in. He trusted what he did know—He knew his God. God called him to go and made these promises:

> And I will make of you a great nation, and I will bless you and make your name great, so that you will be a blessing. I will bless those who bless you, and him who dishonors you I will curse, and in you all the families of the earth shall be blessed. (Genesis 12:2–3)

Abram trusted in a God he could not see and followed where He led. The covenant was initiated by God and did not rest on Abram for it to be fulfilled. The plan could be trusted because God created the plan in the first place and would fulfill His purpose. He chose to use Abram to fulfill His purpose, and knowing his God, Abram chose to follow with complete trust.

Maybe we are not following God to some unknown destination, but God does call us to do the unknown. God created a plan for each of us from the very beginning of time, and much in our lives remains completely unknown to us. God knows what needs to take place in our lives to fulfill the purpose He has for each of us. We cannot always see ahead in His plan, we cannot always know His purpose, but like Abram, God calls us to simply trust.

How is God calling you to walk forward into the unknown? Do you know the plan but not all the steps forward?

_____

_____

_____

_____

Sometimes God does not want you to be concerned with all the steps but just do what is next. Know your God and know that all He calls you to do is simply trust.

UNKNOWN SACRIFICE

Take your son, your only son Isaac, whom you love, and go to the land of Moriah, and offer him there as a burnt offering.

GENESIS 22:2

Outer space has always fascinated me. Star projectors reveal the vastness of space and the brilliance of the hidden stars as they simulate the night sky. The galaxy that includes our solar system is the Milky Way. This barred, spiral galaxy is named because of the hazy band of light that is seen in the sky at night. Though the band can be seen, the individual stars contained in it cannot be seen by the naked eye. Estimated to contain at least one hundred billion stars, the Milky Way is just one of the billions of galaxies in the universe. This means there are potentially thousands of planetary systems like our solar system within the galaxy! Think of all the stars!

As they looked up into the night sky, God made His covenant with Abraham. "And he brought him outside and said, 'Look toward heaven, and number the stars, if you are able to number them.' Then he said to him, 'So shall your offspring be'" (Genesis 15:5).

What an amazing promise this was from God. Impossible as it was to count all the stars, God's promise was shown possible as He provided Isaac to Abraham and Sarah in their old age. Abraham trusted God, leaving his father's house for an unknown place. He also trusted as the plan was known and the promise kept through the birth of Isaac.

But then God made a request of Abraham. God alone could understand the difficulty in what He was asking.

> After these things God tested Abraham and said to him, "Abraham!" And he said, "Here I am." He said, "Take your son, your only son Isaac, whom you love, and go to the land of Moriah, and offer him there as a burnt offering on one of the mountains of which I shall tell you." (Genesis 22:1–2)

The love I have for my own three sons is immeasurable. I can't imagine being asked to make such a sacrifice. Isaac was the son through whom God would make a great nation—more than the stars in the sky, more stars than Abraham could count. God was asking him to sacrifice and suffer the loss of his only son for his belief in God. God was asking him to give up his precious son, showing God was more precious to him.

Abraham was willing. He knew God and trusted that He would be able to bring a great nation from him despite the death of his son. He would be able to accomplish His plan even in ways that were not known to Abraham, so he let go of what was known and trusted God.

Yet God knew fully what He was asking of Abraham because He Himself would give up His only Son completely. He knew that many years later, He would sacrifice His only Son, Jesus, so we would have the opportunity to enjoy eternal life with Him by accepting His gift of salvation. This plan was unknown to Abraham, but God was using Abraham's story as a part of His greater story. Each of us also has a part in God's story. We do not always know what God's plan is. While we can trust what we do know, God is also asking us to trust what we do not know.

Abraham did not know that God would spare his son, Isaac, and fulfill His plan in the original way. He only knew that he would obey God and do whatever He asked because, whether he knew or did not know God's plan, he knew without a doubt he could trust God.

The known can become unknown as God's plan unfolds.
What effect does this have as you trust God? Does it shake your trust?
How can you prepare for changes in direction or a call for unexpected sacrifice?

_____

_____

_____

_____

Step into the unknown,
knowing you serve a God who knows.

UNKNOWN TIMING

By faith Sarah herself received power to conceive, even when she was past the age, since she considered him faithful who had promised.

HEBREWS 11:11

Control—how do I look at control? Not so all goes my way or for a need to be in charge. Instead, to change how things are taking place, so they turn out the "right" way. To fix things for people so everything turns out "the way it should be."

Control is the power to guide or influence a person's behavior or events. However, most often I find out I am not in control ... nor do I need to be.

Despite taking an unknown journey with God as they walked through married life, Sarai and Abram shared life and faith in God. You don't see Sarai questioning Abram as God encouraged them to leave all they knew to follow Him to a new land with His special promise. A woman of great faith and love for her husband, she followed Abraham, and together they followed God's leading. However, Sarai had a faith battle of her own as she continued to age, when the promise of a great nation seemed to become an impossibility.

Knowing God's covenant, Sarai waited ten long years in the land of their inheritance for a baby of her own. God's plan is not unknown to her because He had clearly said in His promise to Abram that he could "'look toward heaven, and number the stars, if you are able to number them.' Then he said to him, 'So shall your offspring be'" (Genesis 15:5). What was unknown to Sarai was how and when His plan would come about.

Sarai decided to move forward with a plan of her own. She tried to orchestrate God's plan as she had Hagar step in to produce an heir, an acceptable custom in the Near East at the time. Genesis reveals the plan:

> Now Sarai, Abram's wife, had borne him no children. She had a female Egyptian servant whose name was Hagar. And Sarai said to Abram, "Behold now, the Lord has prevented me from bearing children. Go in to my servant; it may be that I shall obtain children by her." And Abram listened to the voice of Sarai.
> (Genesis 16:1–2)

However, her plan backfired and caused great heartache. It was not God's plan. Rather than patiently submitting to God and waiting for His perfect timing, Sarai followed her own plan. In creating her plan, Sarai was essentially saying that God's plan was not good enough. His timing was not right. Her plan was better. Sarai quickly learned heartache as her plan unfolded with Hagar bearing a child to Abram, and Sarai's heart filled with jealousy.

God's plan would come to pass in the way He designed the journey. Sarai had to get to the place of trust in God, of releasing her control, and just having faith that He would fulfill His promise in His way and in His timing. Through many years of lessons and growth, Sarai (now Sarah) did come to that place. She learned that following God's unknown path brought blessings she could never have orchestrated.

She is remembered in Hebrews 11:11: "By faith Sarah herself received power to conceive, even when she was past the age, since she considered him faithful who had promised." She was blessed as an entire nation came through her and Abraham—God's special people in God's way and in God's timing.

Control remains best left in the hands of the Creator of the Universe, who knows the end from the beginning. His ways are not our ways, but His ways will always be the best ways.

As you try to make things turn out the "right" way, how does that suggest God is not right?

When things are not the way they "should be," why do you think you need to change them?

What are some steps you can take to release control?

_____

_____

_____

When God is in control, things may not be as we think they should be, but they are how God wants them to be.

UNKNOWN PLAN

*For who has known the mind of the Lord,
or who has been his counselor?*

ROMANS 11:34

Some events have the ability to shake us. We remember so clearly where we were and what we were doing when we heard the news. These unknown happenings, whether good or bad, change the course of life, and we remember the moment.

Those old enough to remember can recall the exact details surrounding them as the events of September 11, 2001, began to unfold. At 8:46 a.m., the North Tower of the World Trade Center in New York City was rocked as American Airlines Flight 11 crashed into its side. Less than twenty minutes later, the South Tower was struck by United Airlines Flight 175. With the second plane striking the towers, it became clear more was taking place than a mere accident. This was confirmed as American Airlines Flight 77 struck the western side of the Pentagon at 9:37 a.m. As the towers were collapsing, United Airlines Flight 93 crashed near Shanksville in the Pennsylvania countryside. America was under attack.

Horror filled the air as quickly as the smoke engulfed people running for their lives from the collapsing towers. Feelings of shock, fear, grief, and sadness filled our nation. The terrorist attacks carried out by al-

Qaeda that morning brought unknown horror as lives were changed forever. These unknown happenings led to an unknown future. Only the evil of the day could be felt, but God uses the unknown and evil to bring about good. And there was good, even in the midst of these attacks.

Flight 93 was scheduled to be an early-morning nonstop flight from Newark, New Jersey, to San Francisco, California, but was delayed at takeoff. As the flight ascended, passengers were alerted to the attacks and began to devise a plan. Though the terrorists were in the process of taking over the flight, the passengers, led by Todd Beamer, retaliated. The hijackers were forced to crash the plane in a field near Indian Lake and Shanksville, Pennsylvania, preventing them from reaching their target. The heroic efforts of Todd Beamer and fellow passengers saved lives.

But why did God allow this evil to take place? Where was He in the chaos? So often when the effects of sin grip our lives and cause incredible heartache, we question God. We forget that His ways are not our ways. In fact, our thoughts and ways are nothing compared to the depth of His knowledge and wisdom as explained by Paul.

> Oh, the depth of the riches and wisdom and knowledge of God! How unsearchable are his judgments and how inscrutable his ways! "For who has known the mind of the Lord, or who has been his counselor?" "Or who has given a gift to him that he might be repaid?" For from him and through him and to him are all things. To him be glory forever. Amen. (Romans 11:33–36)

God is the Creator, Sustainer, and Heir of all things. His wisdom and knowledge are so far above man's and are inscrutable or impossible to understand and interpret. He is God, and we are not. God sometimes will allow things to happen in His wisdom. Nothing is beyond His knowledge. Nothing is unknown to Him. We do not always understand His ways or why He allows things to happen as they do, especially when they lead to such horrible tragedy. We can trust a God who is fully in control, even in the tragedies of this world.

Lisa Beamer, widow of Todd Beamer, quickly became a person of public interest as she worked through the tragic loss of her husband with such grace and strength. Little did she know as Todd quietly kissed her goodbye in the early-morning hours on September 11 that events yet unknown would change her world and lead to an unknown future raising their family alone. Because of Todd's heroic acts, the media sought countless interviews with Lisa. The details of the last moments on Flight 93 and Todd's part in it brought hope and goodness to a nation rocked with fear and loss.

Lisa had many opportunities to share the faith in God she and Todd shared. Knowing the depth of God's wisdom and knowledge had built a firm foundation of trust in her sovereign God. As she described coping with loss, Lisa summed up how she chose to face sorrows and challenges each day in her book *Let's Roll! Ordinary People, Extraordinary Courage*.

> I can sink into depression or anger or anxiety, or I can trust that God is working everything for my good. I have chosen to believe God—to believe he loves me and has a plan for now and for eternity. I don't claim to understand, but I choose daily—even moment by moment—to have faith not in what is seen but in what is unseen. The road ahead is uncertain and even scary at times, but I believe

that God will provide what's best for me, just when I need it.[3]

Good still can result in tragedy and loss. Though at times Lisa still faces the unknown, she faces life with a God who is known. Through tragedy, Lisa has shared her faith in ways she could not have without the unknown events of 9/11 taking place. When all around seems untrustworthy, God can be trusted. Because we can be secure and rely on God's greater wisdom, we can trust Him completely as He leads us over the rough roads of life; we can know we do not have to solve all the mysteries. All He asks is for us to trust Him.

What events in your life have shaken you, causing you to question God?
How is your plan better than His?
What steps do you need to take to trust in God's control of every event in your life?

_____
_____
_____
_____

---

[3] Lisa Beamer with Ken Abraham, *Let's Roll! Ordinary People, Extraordinary Courage*, (Wheaton, Illinois: Tyndale House Publishers), 312.

The only true security in this life comes from placing our trust in the God who loves us and is in complete control of the events of our lives and our world.[4]

---

[4] Lisa Beamer with Ken Abraham, *Let's Roll! Ordinary People, Extraordinary Courage* (Wheaton, Illinois: Tyndale House Publishers, 2022), 269.

TRUST IN KNOWN CIRCUMSTANCES

Knowing what is about to take place should bring me comfort or at least confidence in my next steps, but Lord, I am afraid. I know what is ahead of me, but the results could go either way. In taking this risk, things could get really hard. Please provide me with courage knowing what is ahead, God, and the needed grace as I trust You in every moment.

KNOWN FOR A PURPOSE

What I have said, that I will bring about;
what I have planned, that I will do.

ISAIAH 46:11 NIV

I had the delight of going to probate court to obtain a new car title.

Before my dad went home to be with the Lord, all was in order except for his car. What a process! Have you ever had to work through the complicated paperwork? I had done little to care for his car while he was failing, so not only did it remain in his name at his death, the tags were also expired. Off I went to probate court, which I did not take care of right away. Though I was working through the paperwork, one day I was pulled over for expired tags. The law required the tags to be up to date. I knew this, yet the process through court delayed obtaining new tags. No title, no tags. Still, the law said I could not drive with expired tags. I knew this. It was the law.

Even a queen was under the law. The book of Esther begins with King Ahasuerus giving a feast showing the riches of his kingdom. As the feast came to an end, the drunken king requested Queen Vashti to come before the men to display her beauty. Had he been sober, King Ahasuerus never would have made this foolish request. Queen Vashti knew obeying his request would bring upon her the disrespect of the Persian nation as well as the king himself. She would not go. "But Queen Vashti refused to come at the king's command delivered by the eunuchs. At this the king became enraged, and his anger burned within him" (Esther 1:12).

Upon her refusal, she lost her position as queen. Disobedience to the king's commands was known to be against the law. Queen Vashti was used as an example to the women in their land that it was not okay to refuse their husbands, even in unfair requests. Women were to obey. How sad this was for her, yet God was making the way for His plan and the salvation of His people.

Isaiah describes God's providence in the lives of mankind:

> I am God, and there is no other; I am God, and there is none like me. I make known the end from the beginning, from ancient times, what is still to come. I say, "My purpose will stand, and I will do all that I please." From the east I summon a bird of prey; from a far-off land, a man to fulfill my purpose. What I have said, that I will bring about; what I have planned, that I will do.
> (Isaiah 46:9–11 NIV)

All seems so unfair for Queen Vashti. In disobeying the king's commands, she was going against the law, but she did what she had to do. God uses her story to help us better understand the future risk Esther would take. Her story helps us see the king, his heart, and what Esther would be up against. Queen Vashti's story helps us see God's providential hand working with what Vashti knows to bring about what He needs.

Sometimes situations occur in our lives that seem so unfair to us. We have chosen to follow the wise path, doing everything God asks us to do, but the result is pain and difficulty. Everything leads to heartache and hurt with no good to be seen. Based on everything we knew, we thought our wise choices would make the situation better. However, although we may know the path, this does not guarantee the journey will be easy. We can be assured God will use the information He has given us to lead us through what needs to take place for His purpose to be fulfilled.

How do you respond when you know doing the right thing is going to lead to heartache?
What biblical truths can guide you when what you know suddenly becomes unknown?

_____
_____
_____
_____

When the known becomes unknown, do you trust God, who has always known?

KNOWN WITH A RISK

*And who knows whether you have not come to the
kingdom for such a time as this?*

ESTHER 4:14

A British royal wedding captured the attention of many Americans, causing them to wake up bleary-eyed in the early-morning hours to watch Lady Diana Spencer marry the Prince of Wales. The wedding took place on July 29, 1981, at Saint Paul's Cathedral in London. White garden roses adorned the church, where the doors were thrown open for guests. Dressed in coat and tails and the finest dresses, gathering nobility waited to make their entrance. Perched atop each head was a hat, and for some of the women the choice was a fascinator, a small headpiece adorned with feathers, beads, or flowers. Horses clip-clopped through the crowded street, pulling the glass coach on its way to the church. Elegance graced every part of the beautiful bride as Lady Diana stepped from the coach and entered the church to become a princess. Commoners crowded every road and passageway, looking on as history unfolded.

Esther, herself a commoner—in fact, a Jew, one of God's chosen people—gathered with a group of beautiful young virgins, of which one would be selected to be the next queen. By God's divine plan, Esther was chosen, and Mordecai, her uncle, stayed close to the castle. In doing so, one day Mordecai heard of a plot to take the king's life and reported it, so the king was saved.

A few brief verses share this part of the story and almost seem out of place with the story of Esther as a whole. However, God uses all things.

Next, Haman was elevated to a position of highest authority by the king, and all the royal officials knelt to pay homage to him. However, Mordecai would not kneel. Because Mordecai would not pay homage by kneeling, Haman wanted to destroy not only Mordecai but all the Jewish people. How quickly the day changed for the people as they learned of the edict of the king, designed by Haman, that would bring about their destruction.

With God, though, there is always hope, even when it seems there isn't.

So life became hard for Queen Esther. In making her aware of the edict, Mordecai asked her to go before the king and beg his favor. Queen Esther knew her circumstances. She could lose her life simply for going before the king without being summoned. She reminded Mordecai of the risk, but Mordecai reminded her of the greater risk.

> Then Mordecai told them to reply to Esther, "Do not think to yourself that in the king's palace you will escape any more than all the other Jews. For if you keep silent at this time, relief and deliverance will rise for the Jews from another place, but you and your father's house will perish. And who knows whether you have not come to the kingdom for such a time as this?" (Esther 4:13–14)

Even if Queen Esther did not take this risk, her life would still be in jeopardy when the edict was fulfilled. She would die in the end. Her refusal would not keep the Lord from His purpose; deliverance would come. But Queen Esther would miss out on the blessing of being used by God for His people. She knew her God and the love He had for His people. While God could find another way, He had changed Esther's position from a commoner to a queen for this time. God opened this door for Esther for such a time as this.

God gives each of us opportunities; however, if we choose to not be used in His plan, He will find someone who is willing. God's plan for us sometimes involves known risk, and we don't always see the unknown opportunities that may arise from the risk. Sometimes the difficulty we experience causes us to seek understanding and cry out, *How long?* Trust comes in knowing we are where God needs us to be to fulfill the purpose He has created us to fulfill.

Risk takes courage. How do you prepare yourself to step out in courage and follow God?
How has obedience to God's difficult tasks changed you?

_____
_____
_____
_____

God sees all things and only asks us to trust Him for such a time as this.

KNOWN TO MOVE FORWARD

Let me hear in the morning of your steadfast love, for in you I trust. Make me know the way I should go, for to you I lift up my soul.

PSALM 143:8

My dad went home to be with the Lord in October 2021. With his passing, I was alone in the world. My brother and mom had both gone to heaven years before, and I was the last one left of my immediate family. It was an incredibly lonely feeling. I felt so lost. I wasn't sure what to do next, where to go. Have you ever felt that way? Lost, alone, not sure which way to turn or what the path was to move forward. Queen Esther must have experienced some of these feelings knowing she was soon to stand before her king and possibly be rejected and killed.

Queen Esther chose to follow God's leading and do what He called her to do. She knew she needed strength and courage for this task, which would only come from God. She knew she needed time with Him and the support of those around her. She could not do it alone, not without Him. With her court, she spent three days going before God, seeking His hand, as seen by her command:

> Go, gather all the Jews to be found in Susa, and hold a fast on my behalf, and do not eat or drink for three days,

night or day. I and my young women will also fast as you do. Then I will go to the king, though it is against the law, and if I perish, I perish. (Esther 4:16)

God's hand upheld Queen Esther as she went before the king several days later. With courage and strength, she could approach him. She trusted God's plan; His will would come to pass, even in her death. However, King Ahasuerus's response was amazing. Not only did he hold out his scepter but offered her half the kingdom, readily accepting her dinner invitation for himself and Haman.

While planning and hosting two royal dinners, Queen Esther patiently waited for God's guidance in revealing Haman's evil ways. She showed patience and grace as she planned how to bring the plot before the king. King Ahasuerus was willing to grant her the request from the start, but the queen held back. She didn't use the position she held to get what she wanted, and she didn't tattle on Haman to get her way or to have vengeance. An evil had been done, and Queen Esther carefully presented the issue. Her motives would be clear to the king: she wanted to save her people.

Throughout this story, Queen Esther knew what was at stake. She also knew that she had a job to do. If she did not risk herself, her people would be at risk. She knew more and more that her risk was little compared with God's plans. She also knew that she could not fulfill His plan without His guidance, wisdom, and strength. She sought Him completely, and as she and those around her spent time fasting and praying before the Lord, they were filled with Him. I imagine her sharing the prayer of David: "Let me hear in the morning of your steadfast love, for in you I trust. Make me know the way I should go, for to you I lift up my soul" (Psalm 143:8).

Queen Esther knew the way to move forward in the coming days because she allowed God to show her the way to go. She was assured of His never-ending love, and she trusted God completely. She spent time with Him, and He gave her the courage to move forward with the plan He had for her.

Like Queen Esther, we can be put in situations where we know we need to respond. We are required to act, but we have no clue where to start or which way to turn. We feel lost and unsure. The path forward seems insurmountable. In His never-ending love, God faithfully guides us along the next steps. He gives us the courage to do what He needs us to do. We just need to allow Him to show us the way.

Do you wait for something to go wrong before you go to the Lord? Why?

When the way is unclear or full of fear, what steps can you take to seek God first?

Queen Esther had a plan to seek God's help. What is your plan when you have hard decisions to make?

_____

_____

_____

_____

Hear in the morning and be reminded of God's steadfast love.

KNOWN YET CONFIDENT

*He only is my rock and my salvation, my fortress;
I shall not be shaken.*

PSALM 62:6

Launching from the Kennedy Space Center in Florida on April 11, 1970, Apollo 13 was the seventh crewed mission and the third craft meant to land on the moon in the Apollo space program. The goal of this mission was to demonstrate precision in landing and to explore specific sites on the moon. However, the goal quickly changed from exploration to rescue when an explosion resulted from a routine stirring of oxygen tanks. With the lunar module becoming the lifeboat for the astronauts, the NASA team worked to bring the crew home alive. NASA showed teamwork and camaraderie as they recalculated and worked through replacing the oxygen that had leaked into space.

The world united in mutual concern and prayer as they watched the potential disaster unfold. While NASA used what they knew to turn from a successful mission to a rescue mission, much was out of their hands. They could only do so much and wait. The agonizing wait finally ended as contact was restored and the astronauts splashed down safely in the South Pacific Ocean. Jim Lovell, commander of Apollo 13, called the mission a "successful failure." The mission became a success because of the saved lives.

Salvation came to Queen Esther and the Jewish people when Haman was found out and lost his life for his evil plot. What seemed a victory soon returned to tragedy with the remembrance of the edict yet to be fulfilled. You see, according to Persian law, no edict of a Persian king could be revoked. The edict written and sealed by Haman in the name of King Ahasuerus was still in effect. This known situation was out of their hands, so once again, Esther brought it before the king. Knowing she potentially faced death, Queen Esther, submitting to God's will, came before the king in quiet confidence. Again appearing before the king without a summons, this time she was backed by God's grace and strength that had brought her through the first time.

Sometimes God takes us through the same hardship several times to accomplish His purposes. He gives us grace each time. As David waited in quietness for God's work to be accomplished, peace flowed over him:

> For God alone, O my soul, wait in silence, for my hope is from him. He only is my rock and my salvation, my fortress; I shall not be shaken. On God rests my salvation and my glory; my mighty rock, my refuge is God. Trust in him at all times, O people; pour out your heart before him; God is a refuge for us. (Psalm 62:5–8)

Esther, though troubled by the predicament of her people, knew she would rest in God's plan. Although she might again have been laying her life on the line, in God was the safe place to be. Spending time with God renewed her faith in Him and fixed her heart on the work He had for her to do. Quiet submission and confidence took place. King Ahasuerus, holding out his scepter and sparing her life, listened to her plea. A new edict was issued. Tragedy was again turned to victory as the people were saved.

Multiple times Queen Esther was called upon to step forward in faith knowing what could take place. Through time spent with God, she knew that even if her life was lost, following God was the only option for her. She could rest in His plan for herself and her people knowing that whatever took place, God's purpose would be accomplished.

Confidence in God's plan for our lives always strengthens as we spend time with Him and learn more of His character. When we face difficult situations and see how God brings us through those difficulties, it lays a foundation of strength and confidence in Him to face whatever comes next. Sometimes God asks us to face hardships one after the other. He never promised life would be easy, but He did promise to be our refuge, our strength, our ever-present help in times of trouble. Because we know this to be true, we can step forward in the same quiet submission and confidence that Queen Esther did.

Where do your thoughts take you when the hardship keeps coming?
How has God shown Himself through these difficulties?
In what ways has God helped you lay a foundation of confidence and strength in Him?

_____
_____
_____
_____

Knowing the situation only gives knowledge.
Knowing God gives quiet confidence and trust in Him.

TRUST IN UNFAIR CIRCUMSTANCES

Lord, I don't know what to say. I can't believe she's gone. She died so young, before she had a chance to really live. It seems so unfair. What words of comfort can I bring? Not my words, but Yours. You show through the heartache and loss that the testimony she gave for You in her life continues through her death. You remind me that when all is unfair, I can trust You in every moment.

UNFAIR AND DID NOTHING

For your steadfast love is before my eyes,
and I walk in your faithfulness.

PSALM 26:3

How is this fair? A job is offered simply because you are a sister, a nephew, or a friend. This happens in businesses, with celebrities in Hollywood, on school teams, even in churches. Nepotism can cause those more qualified to be left aside, fostering mistrust and resentment. The practice is unfair to those who work hard to advance. Those chosen for the job were special, privileged, favored—or should we say favorites? But what about the others? Those maybe more qualified?

Joseph was the favorite. In a family of twelve brothers, he was the special favorite of his father, Jacob. Jacob made this very clear as he showed Joseph special love in giving him a coat of many colors. Always hoping to find some kind of favor in Jacob's eyes, Joseph's brothers fought feelings of resentment. Their emotions boiled. "But when his brothers saw that their father loved him more than all his brothers, they hated him and could not speak peacefully to him" (Genesis 37:4).

Not helping the situation, Joseph relayed two of his dreams to them. In one, eleven sheaves of wheat bowed down to his sheaf of wheat. In the other, the sun, the moon, and eleven—yes eleven—stars bowed down to Joseph. Even Jacob felt Joseph was pushing things a bit.

One day, Jacob sent Joseph to check on his brothers as they pastured their sheep near Shechem. Seeing Joseph coming, the brothers quickly put together a plot to take his life. Reuben came to his rescue by suggesting they throw Joseph into a pit instead, hoping to return Joseph to their father later. The brothers agreed to this plan, and Joseph soon found himself in an empty pit. While Reuben was away, however, the brothers pulled Joseph from the pit and sold him to Midianites headed to Egypt.

Joseph had done nothing to deserve such treatment, yet here he was on his way to Egypt. His world had turned upside down. He later recognized the wrong his brothers had done: "For I was indeed stolen out of the land of the Hebrews, and here also I have done nothing that they should put me into the pit" (Genesis 40:15). He cast no blame. I imagine he talked of the unfairness of his situation with the Lord. Throughout his life, Joseph was dealt an incredibly hard hand he had no choice in, no control over, yet he trusted God completely. He had to have struggled. Who wouldn't? Yet he trusted in what he knew about God. Joseph chose faith rather than bitterness, trust in God's sovereignty rather than revenge. He held on to God when life spun out of control.

Our lives can bring us along a similar path. We can be treated unfairly or put into situations we have no choice in and no control over. Our lives can be completely turned upside down through the choices of others in a matter of minutes. Circumstances change, and suddenly life seems out of control.

Remember David's declaration in Psalm 26:1–3: "Vindicate me, O Lord, for I have walked in my integrity, and I have trusted in the Lord without wavering. Prove me, O Lord, and try me; test my heart and my mind. For your steadfast love is before my eyes, and I walk in your faithfulness."

What will you choose? Will you choose faith or bitterness, trust in a sovereign God, or revenge? When life begins to spin, what will you hold to?

What events have caused your life to suddenly spin out of control?
What choices are you making as you process your emotions?
How will you respond to those who brought the hurt?

_____
_____
_____
_____

When life spins out of control,
put your hand in the One who holds control.

UNFAIR AND FALSELY ACCUSED

*In return for my love they accuse me,
but I give myself to prayer.*

PSALM 109:4

Have you ever been accused of committing an act or sharing words you had no part of? You know you are completely innocent, but everything is stacked against you, making you look guilty. Innocent until proven guilty—the legal basis for this statement is shown in the Fifth, Sixth, and Fourteenth Amendments to the Constitution of our country. We expect even in our daily lives that we are not considered guilty of something unless it is proved we have done the wrong. Yet sometimes life brings false accusations, and you are treated as guilty until proven innocent.

Joseph adjusted to life in Egypt after being sold to Potiphar, the captain of the guard. In fact, God so blessed Joseph that Potiphar's house was also blessed.

> The Lord was with Joseph, and he became a successful man, and he was in the house of his Egyptian master. His master saw that the Lord was with him and that the Lord

caused all that he did to succeed in his hands. So Joseph found favor in his sight and attended him, and he made him overseer of his house and put him in charge of all that he had. (Genesis 39:2–4)

Potiphar gave all that he had into Joseph's hands, except for his wife. Potiphar's wife saw Joseph and wanted him. She asked many times for Joseph to come lie with her. Even after Joseph's constant refusals, while alone in the house one day she insisted one more time. Joseph again refused. "How then can I do this great wickedness and sin against God?" (Genesis 39:9). Leaving everything, Joseph fled.

Being obedient to God was so much more important to him than the pleasure of sin. Though innocent, Joseph was falsely accused as Potiphar's wife lied to her husband. In most cases, the sentence for this accusation would have been death; instead, Potiphar had Joseph thrown into the royal prison. Maybe Potiphar doubted some of his wife's story; we will never know. Joseph was thrown into prison and into another unfair situation—unfair and falsely accused.

Psalm 109 recounts a time when David dealt with false accusations. He had not provoked or contributed to his circumstances, which made him feel more acutely the wrongs done to him. He responded to his attacks: "In return for my love they accuse me, but I give myself to prayer" (v. 4). He committed his difficulties to God in prayer and left the results in God's hands.

Once again in the life of Joseph, there was no evidence of bitterness in his heart for the false accusations at the hand of Potiphar's wife. Joseph trusted that God would take care of him even though the truth wasn't being seen. He overlooked their offenses and forgave them. He waited on God in prison and continued to serve Him. The Lord continued to be with him. Genesis 39 closes with God blessing Joseph and giving him favor with the keeper of the prison. Joseph made God his refuge. He honored God with his obedience and let God take care of his honor.

Unfair situations in life come in many ways, but they are especially hard to take when you are falsely accused, when you are blamed, when you are completely innocent. A natural response would be to stand up for yourself and prove your innocence. The easy response would be to seek revenge on those who falsely accused you. The more difficult response would be to overlook the offense and forgive as God forgives our many offenses. God is not blind to the unfairness and false accusations of this world. Rather than taking care of those who are against us, take it to the One who will stand up for our innocence and make things right.

What steps can be set in place to keep you away from questionable situations?

Emotions swirl wildly when you are falsely accused. How can you bring about a godly response?

_____

_____

_____

_____

Responding with grace and love brings blessing and healing not only to yourself but to those around you.

UNFAIR AND FORGOTTEN

*"For," he said, "God has made me forget all my
hardship and all my father's house."*

GENESIS 41:51

Looking out the window into the darkness, I scanned the woods for signs of life. An eerie noise startled the peaceful quiet. Jumping back, I trembled from head to toe as I stared into the face of a bat seeking its way in.

Then I awoke, so thankful to find I was not face-to-face with a bat! My great fear of bats even keeps me from looking at them from a distance at the zoo. When nighttime skies bring them swooping, I run for cover. Needless to say, I was thankful to find this bat was only in my dreams.

In the times of the Old and New Testaments, God used dreams to reveal His truth to His prophets and others. Dreams often foretold the future. Genesis 40 continues Joseph's story in prison, where God used him to interpret the dreams of men from Pharoah's royal court.

Joseph was quickly trusted by the keeper of the prison and put in charge of many things. As time went on, the royal prison gained two new prisoners, the king's cupbearer and the baker. Both had committed offenses against Pharoah. One evening both dreamed dreams that troubled them greatly. Seeing the struggle in both men, Joseph offered to find meaning, knowing God would provide him the interpretation for each man's dream. For the cupbearer, Joseph shared a message of restoration and in return asked that the cupbearer remember him before Pharaoh. The baker's dream interpretation foretold the man's death.

Joseph was forgotten by the cupbearer but continued where God placed him. Hope had blossomed in his prison darkness with the cupbearer's promise, but with no response the hope faded.

One night the Pharaoh dreamed. Finally remembered by the cupbearer, Joseph was summoned and by God's grace interpreted the dreams, revealing God's plans of years of plenty followed by famine. Joseph not only interpreted the Pharaoh's dreams but shared godly wisdom on how to handle the coming years. In an amazing turn of events, the Pharaoh responded. "Then Pharaoh said to Joseph, 'Since God has shown you all this, there is none so discerning and wise as you are. You shall be over my house, and all my people shall order themselves as you command. Only as regards the throne will I be greater than you'" (Genesis 41:39–40).

Joseph's life was changed as he led Egypt through the years of plenty and of famine. He married and was blessed with two sons, Manasseh and Ephraim. "Joseph called the name of the firstborn Manasseh. 'For,' he said, 'God has made me forget all my hardship and all my father's house'" (Genesis 41:51).

Joseph had been forgotten, yet God also helped him forget. He didn't hold on to the past and allow that to cloud his future. Joseph trusted God with his past, present, and future. His complete trust in God's plan for his life allowed him to let go of any hurt or heartache from the unfairness of his life that could have settled in his heart. He was able to look through his life and see how God had brought him through the unfair difficulties to this place. He forgot the hard times as suggested by Manasseh's name. Joseph's heart was also revealed with the meaning of Ephraim. "The name of the second he called Ephraim, 'For God has made me fruitful in the land of my affliction'" (Genesis 41:52).

We can feel forgotten and unimportant too. Events in our past have traumatized and changed us, and we have a difficult time knowing how to live in the present, let alone think of the future. When we find forgiveness for ourselves or others, we often see how God uses troubles in the past to prepare us for the present so we can face the future. Before we were even born, God already knew the beautiful masterpiece we would be in eternity. While He does not cause us to sin, He uses sin and all the difficulties, as well as all the beautiful experiences in our life, to shape us into the masterpiece He already sees us to be. He knows what needs to take place in our lives. Letting go of difficulties and extending forgiveness for past hurts or mistakes allow you to see God's hand as He teaches, molds, and shapes you. Seeking His guidance in the present will lead you toward His plan enfolding before you.

How do you feel forgotten or unimportant?
What steps do you need to take to forget and let go?

_____

_____

_____

_____

Look to the past and see God's hand. Live in the present and cling to His guiding hand. Trust that your future is held in His sovereign hand.

UNFAIR YET GOOD

As for you, you meant evil against me, but God meant it for good, to bring it about that many people should be kept alive, as they are today.

GENESIS 50:20

Do you ever have times when you just don't know what to say? Eyes swim with tears as trembling voices express the heartache of miscarriage, the breakup of a long-desired engagement, the betrayal of a friend, sickness that takes a parent away. Dreams fall apart, yet all around, best friends experience these same dreams fulfilled, and all is going well. Life can be so unfair. What do you say as the tears begin to stream down their cheeks? Why was the dream not good enough for them? Had they done something wrong?

My thoughts go back to Joseph and the many, many years of unfairness. He must have had thoughts of what his life would be like. Each time life seemed to be looking up, a weird twist would come, and another dream was dashed. The response of his heart gave evidence of his time with the Lord. The twists and turns could have led him to frustration, anger, and bitterness. But he chose to trust. He caused nothing, could control nothing, yet his attitude through it all was one of trusting his sovereign God.

By the end of the book of Genesis, Jacob had died, and again feelings of guilt swept over Joseph's brothers as they recalled the unfair life they had caused their brother, Joseph. But Joseph had already extended his forgiveness to them.

> And God sent me before you to preserve for you a remnant on earth, and to keep alive for you many survivors. So it was not you who sent me here, but God. He has made me a father to Pharaoh, and lord of all his house and ruler over all the land of Egypt. (Genesis 45:7–8)

Joseph could forgive his brothers because it wasn't their wrong that led him to the unfair place he was in. Their wrong led Joseph to the right place where God needed him to be. Unforgiveness would have stepped in the way of God's plan.

So again, with Jacob's death, they needed reassurance of Joseph's forgiveness. Joseph again offered this forgiveness. "But Joseph said to them, 'Do not fear, for am I in the place of God? As for you, you meant evil against me, but God meant it for good, to bring it about that many people should be kept alive, as they are today'" (Genesis 50:19–20).

Joseph lived his life from the beginning to the end with complete trust in God no matter what he faced. He went through hard and unfair circumstances and suffered from the mistakes and sins of others, yet God used each part of his journey to bring about good.

To the one suffering a miscarriage, a failed relationship, the loss of a dream, the answer is the same: trust God. Trust allows us to place the hurt and heartache in the hands of the One who sees the good it will bring about in the lives of those around us. The hurt and heartache of those unfulfilled dreams shape us to be God's vessel to minister to even one in a way we couldn't have if that dream had been fulfilled.

God will use each part of your journey to help you reach another in a way you couldn't have before. Not only will this minister to them in their struggle, but you will be blessed by being a vessel for Him. God will be glorified as others see Him through your experiences.

How have you experienced unfair loss or betrayal?
What is the response of your heart?
In what ways can you allow God to use it to help others?

_____
_____
_____
_____

> *Trust the One who knows the path to achieve the purpose*
> *He knows will fulfill His perfect plan.*

TRUST IN THE IMPOSSIBLE

It's not supposed to be this way! I just don't know how to fix it. I can't fix it. This is impossible, Lord! What should I do? There is no way out of this mess. Please show me what to do. As I ask, I remember. You, Lord, caused Peter to walk on the water. You made the seemingly impossible possible as he walked to You. Nothing is impossible with You, so I can trust You in every moment.

HUMBLY ACCEPTING THE IMPOSSIBLE

Behold, I am the servant of the Lord; let it be to me according to your word.

LUKE 1:38

Impossibilities: something that cannot be undone or happen.

- A newborn running across the floor.
- Time travel.
- Changing another person's heart.
- Fitting a camel through the eye of a needle.
- Moving a mountain.

What seems impossible to you?

The angel Gabriel was sent by God to Galilee to share a message with Mary.

> And he came to her and said, "Greetings, O favored one, the Lord is with you!" But she was greatly troubled at the saying, and tried to discern what sort of greeting this might be. And the angel said to her, "Do not be afraid,

Mary, for you have found favor with God. And behold, you will conceive in your womb and bear a son, and you shall call his name Jesus. He will be great and will be called the Son of the Most High. And the Lord God will give to him the throne of his father David, and he will reign over the house of Jacob forever, and of his kingdom there will be no end." (Luke 1:28–33)

So many thoughts and emotions must have passed through Mary as she took in this greeting. An angel of God suddenly appeared before her! One just didn't get visited by an angel very often. Mary knew it meant something, and in a mixture of confusion, anxiety, and concern, she listened to the angel's message. Upon hearing his message came the realization of the impossibility before her. Bear a son? How could she bear a son? Mary was betrothed to Joseph, but they had never been intimate. Puzzled, Mary asked, "How will this be, since I am a virgin?" (Luke 1:34)

Gabriel assured Mary that she would not conceive through natural means but through a supernatural miracle of the Holy Spirit. While this assurance did not give her understanding, knowing this extraordinary event would be orchestrated by God's hand, Mary trusted. God was able to accomplish what was considered impossible to fulfill His divine plan. Mary's response shows quiet heroism. "And Mary said, 'Behold, I am the servant of the Lord; let it be to me according to your word.' And the angel departed from her" (Luke 1:38).

In her humble acceptance by faith, Mary fully realized God's plan could lead to divorce, ostracism, suffering, and possible death, yet she recognized the will of God and accepted it. In her deep love for the Lord, she obediently followed what He called her to do.

Mary got there so quickly. She trusted in her sovereign God even before Jesus was born. It didn't take her months and months to get there. She couldn't possibly understand all the pieces of her puzzle. No one had ever experienced pregnancy the way she would. No one would experience the fallout she and Joseph would as the result of God's work. Even before she experienced what would be, she simply trusted and praised the Lord despite what could be. She didn't dwell on what was or what could be based on what she knew; she just trusted God.

While I do not think anyone will ever face an impossible situation quite like Mary's, we do face seemingly impossible situations. Life just seems so hard. Nothing will ever change, and there is no way out. We question why God would have us experience such hardship. We wonder how the situation could ever be made right. We seek to understand how to fit the puzzle pieces of our life together, yet the pieces just don't fit. They seem to be from a different puzzle. Not only has God designed the puzzle of our lives, but He knows the order of the pieces and how they fit together to build the complete picture. God alone makes possible what seems impossible.

What areas of your life seem impossible to you?
What steps can you take to strengthen your faith and leave your pieces with the puzzle maker?

_____

_____

_____

_____

Trusting the God of impossibilities makes our impossible become His possible.

COMPARING THE IMPOSSIBLE

For nothing will be impossible with God.
LUKE 1:37

A simple prayer was offered when everything seemed possible. Newly married to Zechariah, a priest from the division of Abijah, Elizabeth prayed for the blessing of a child. They waited, and the years rolled by. Though they were happy in their life together, as they advanced in years, Elizabeth's barrenness became apparent. There would be no children. The prayer once prayed became an impossibility.

As seen with Mary, the angel Gabriel delivered God's good news. His divine plan would be accomplished through two unusual pregnancies. While serving in the temple, Gabriel appeared to Zechariah. Seeing his fear, Gabriel comforted him with this message: "Do not be afraid, Zechariah, for your prayer has been heard, and your wife Elizabeth will bear you a son, and you shall call his name John" (Luke 1:13).

Their prayer had been heard! Rather than excitement for a dream fulfilled, Zechariah responds with *how?* Similar to Mary's, yet not the same.

- Zechariah: "How can I be sure of this? I am an old man, and my wife is well along in years."
- Mary: "How will this be ... since I am a virgin."

Both asked how, but Mary's how carried with it the inevitable that yes, what the angel said would happen. Zechariah's how was more: Is it able to happen? In The Message his response is translated, "Do you expect me to believe this? I'm an old man and my wife is an old woman" (Luke 1:18 MSG). He did not trust God. Seeing and hearing Gabriel—the angel of the Lord sent by God Himself to deliver this special message—was not enough to help him believe that God could do the impossible. Because Zechariah did not believe the angel's words, through God's power Gabriel performed a miracle until the planned miracle would occur: Zechariah would be unable to speak until his promised son was born.

In their lives, Zechariah and Elizabeth walked blamelessly before the Lord. Just as Mary had been highly favored by God to bear His Son, Zechariah and Elizabeth were specially chosen to bring John into the world to prepare the way of the Lord. Upon finding herself with child, Elizabeth's response was "Thus the Lord has done for me in the days when he looked on me, to take away my reproach among people" (Luke 1:25).

When John was born and his name declared, people questioned Elizabeth's choice. She knew God had done the impossible, and she would follow His plan completely, including using the God-given name. As Zechariah confirmed John's name to the people, his tongue was loosened, and he spoke, blessing God.

Unlike Mary, Zechariah did not trust God in the impossible right away. He had his eyes on the problems of old age and Elizabeth's barrenness. He had long ago given up on his dream of a child, and fulfillment had become an impossibility. Both Zechariah and Mary asked how. But Mary confidently placed her wonder in the God of impossibilities.

We ask how. As we make requests before God in prayer, we know with God all things are possible, but when days, months, and years go by, the unanswered possibilities become impossible in our eyes. So often we place our focus on what makes a situation impossible rather than focusing on what God can do. We look at the problems we see and determine God is not able to take care of a situation with so many obstacles. We come to God when the doors start to open with an attitude: *Do you expect me to believe this?* We forget who God is and what He can do. We no longer see how the possible could happen, let alone the impossible, and we ask how.

When you ask, have confidence as you remember that God is not just a God of the possible but also of the impossible. He is able to make all things happen according to His will. Trust that His path will take you through the impossible and show you that all things are possible because of Him.

In your situation, what problems keep you from believing God could make it possible?

What heart changes need to take place to cause you to trust God in what seems impossible?

_____

_____

_____

_____

*The question is not God's ability,
but our ability to trust His will as we face the impossible.*

MOVING FORWARD IN THE IMPOSSIBLE

When Joseph woke from sleep, he did as the angel of the Lord commanded him: he took his wife.

MATTHEW 1:24

Sometimes I look at the things that happen in my life or the things happening in people around me and think, *This is not how it is supposed to be.* Have you ever felt that way? Marriages are supposed to bring happiness and last till death do us part. Doctors are supposed to diagnose illnesses and prescribe treatment that leads to good health. Believers are supposed to come at issues with grace and love, working through difficulties. These problems become impossible, leading us to think, *This is not how it is supposed to be.*

So many thoughts must have crossed Joseph's mind as he heard that Mary was pregnant. His whole life was opening before him as he prepared for a loving marriage and a shared life with Mary—and then this news. His life was definitely not how it was supposed to be as this impossible situation opened up before him.

Matthew begins the story:

> Now the birth of Jesus Christ took place in this way. When his mother Mary had been betrothed to Joseph,

> before they came together she was found to be with child from the Holy Spirit. And her husband Joseph, being a just man and unwilling to put her to shame, resolved to divorce her quietly. (Matthew 1:18–19)

Joseph was greatly troubled. He was a moral man, and he knew now he could not take Mary as his wife. Of course he assumed she had been unfaithful to him; however, he did not wish for her to go through public disgrace. No, this was not how it was supposed to be, and Joseph tried to think through how to make it right. What would be expected of him as he dealt with Mary's pregnancy? He truly loved her. I'm sure he did not understand why all this was taking place, but he never seemed angry. Instead, his response toward what he thought she had done was filled with love as he didn't want her to be shamed. Joseph wanted all he was supposed to do to rectify the situation to be done in secret.

And then the angel of the Lord appeared to him in a dream.

> But as he considered these things, behold, an angel of the Lord appeared to him in a dream, saying, "Joseph, son of David, do not fear to take Mary as your wife, for that which is conceived in her is from the Holy Spirit. She will bear a son, and you shall call his name Jesus, for he will save his people from their sins." (Matthew 1:20–21)

He had direct communication from God, and while we don't know Joseph's exact reaction, we do know that he did what the angel of the Lord told him to do and took Mary as his wife. Joseph was a godly man. He did not hesitate to do what God called him to do even though he knew it was not how it was supposed to be. Nothing in what God was asking him and Mary to do was normal, but it was God's plan, and

MOVING FORWARD IN THE IMPOSSIBLE

Joseph trusted God completely. Just like Mary, once he knew the voice of the Lord, he moved forward in complete obedience. The impossible became possible. What relief Joseph must have felt to know that, though his path forward was different from what he had expected it would be, God's plan for him still included Mary and the extra gift of together raising the Son of God.

Life has a way of throwing curveballs at us. We set basic expectations of how marriages, careers, children, friendships, and even church life play out. We dream big and set our sights high, believing our dreams will be fulfilled, and life will turn out as planned. Then reality creeps in, and we look around us as expectations go unfulfilled. Dreams are shattered. We pick up the pieces and try to figure life out. Nothing turned out the way we thought it would, and somehow, we need to make life work.

So what should your response be? As you take your cares before the Lord, He will guide you in what you should do. Like Joseph, do not hesitate to do what He calls you to do, even though you know it is not how it is supposed to be. Keep trusting the plan God puts before you, knowing His plan is the perfect plan. You may be surprised by the blessing that comes from how it was not supposed to be.

How do you react when life doesn't work out as planned?
What dreams or expectations do you need to let go of?
How do you prepare your heart to face what's not supposed to be?

_____

_____

_____

_____

No, things are not always as they are supposed to be, but they are how God wants them to be.

EYES ON THE IMPOSSIBLE

But when he saw the wind he was afraid, and beginning to sink he cried out, "Lord, save me."

MATTHEW 14:30

I have always enjoyed swimming. One afternoon, when I was around six, a group of my mom's friends with their children gathered at a home with an above-ground pool. The shimmering water and the refreshing coolness it promised captivated me. Before I knew it, I had fallen in! With minimal swimming skills, I panicked and started to sink. Thankfully, a nearby arm grabbed me up, sweeping me into the safety of my mother's arms. Without proper swimming skills to stay afloat, our bodies sink beneath the surface, proving we cannot walk on water.

Jesus sent the disciples across to the opposite shore in a boat. After speaking to crowds, He needed to spend time with His Father. Jesus went by himself to a mountain to pray. As the disciples headed across the waters, an unexpected windstorm quickly developed, bringing fierce winds that swept them to the middle of the lake. Late in the night, the disciples cried out in alarm as what they perceived to be a ghost was making its way toward them!

But it was Jesus. He was walking on the water to join them. Knowing their fear, Jesus immediately calmed the disciples, saying, "Take heart; it is I. Do not be afraid" (Matthew 14:27).

Recognizing this was Jesus, Peter just wanted to be with Him. Trusting the Lord's power and authority over creation, Peter knew that not only could Jesus walk on the water, but He could help Peter walk on the water. What was impossible for man was possible for Jesus. So Peter put out the request. "And Peter answered him, 'Lord, if it is you, command me to come to you on the water.' He said, 'Come.' So Peter got out of the boat and walked on the water and came to Jesus" (Matthew 14:28–29).

Not only did Peter see the impossible made possible right before his eyes, but Peter also experienced the impossible becoming possible as he himself walked on the water to go to Jesus. When we look to God, what may seem impossible becomes possible when it is according to His plan. But that's just it. We must look to God, and so often we, too, experience what Peter did next. "But when he saw the wind, he was afraid, and beginning to sink he cried out, 'Lord, save me'" (v. 30).

With the squalls raging around him, Peter took his eyes off the object of his faith—Jesus. The storm and the whirling waters caught his attention, causing him to stumble in his faith. He quit relying on the solid foundation of Christ and began to sink.

Like Peter, we can take our eyes off Jesus and allow the storms raging around us to capture our attention. Often we put our faith in a person or rely on circumstances, and everything falls apart. Circumstances change, and people fail us. Jesus will never fail. With Him as the object of our faith, we have a sure foundation. Peter knew this through seeing and experiencing Jesus making the impossible possible. If he didn't have faith in Jesus, he never would have asked to walk to Him. However, like Peter in our humanness, we forget what we know and sink as our faith weakens.

What Peter did next, though, reminds us of what we all should do: cry out to Jesus. Fix your eyes back on Him, and allow Him to hold you through the storms of life. Even in times when your trust is weakest and all looks impossible, Jesus wants you to reach out your hands in faith and hold on to Him. He is already reaching out His hand to grasp on to you. Lift up your eyes, and in faith, hold on to Him.

Where does your faith lie? In your circumstances or in another person?
How have you taken your eyes off Him?

_____

_____

_____

_____

As with Peter, Jesus asks us, "Why did you doubt?"
Keep your eyes focused on the One who makes
possibilities out of impossibilities.

TRUST WHEN YOU ARE CALLED

Oh Lord, what are you asking of me? I have tried to live a life of obedience to You, but this? How can you ask me to do this? It's not that I don't want to; I'm just not sure if I can. I am not ready. I don't have what it takes to do this. But You have what it takes. You will give me what I need to fulfill what You are calling me to do, and I will trust You in every moment.

CALLED WITH PROOF

I am the Lord; I have called you in righteousness;
I will take you by the hand and keep you.

ISAIAH 42:6

Dropping my daughter, Bethany, off at summer camp, I was delighted with her excitement at returning for another year of friends, chapel, worship songs, water activities, and biscuits and gravy. Yes, biscuits and gravy, one of her camp favorites. After greeting the director and my friends on staff, I met and talked with her counselor and then left for home. When I returned on Saturday to take Bethany home, her counselor requested to see my driver's license before I could claim my daughter. She needed proof that I was who I said I was, even though we had met and had a conversation just a week before. She needed proof.

Judges 6–8 continues Israel's history. The children of Israel had again fallen into sin. God had placed them under the control of the Midianites, and in realization of their sin, the Israelites sought God's forgiveness. God chose a man named Gideon to be His instrument to deliver the people from the oppression of these enemies. While hiding from the Midianites threshing wheat, Gideon was approached by the angel of the Lord.

Highlights from their back-and-forth conversation went something like this:

> And the angel of the Lord appeared to him and said to him, "The Lord is with you, O mighty man of valor."
>
> And Gideon said to him, "Please, my lord, if the Lord is with us, why then has all this happened to us?" ...
>
> And the Lord turned to him and said, "... Do not I send you?"
>
> And he said to him, "Please, Lord, how can I save Israel?"
>
> And the Lord said to him, "But I will be with you, and you shall strike the Midianites as one man."
>
> And he said to him, "If now I have found favor in your eyes, then show me a sign that it is you who speak with me." (Judges 6:12–17, quotes abbreviated)

Gideon needed proof. He needed a sign that God was who He said He was. Gideon felt so inadequate for the task God had assigned to him, and he needed to know God's hand was in it. The angel had Gideon prepare an offering and place it upon a rock. As the angel reached out the tip of his staff and touched the meat and cakes, fire sprang from the rock and consumed them. Having provided the proof, the angel disappeared.

Further along, after destroying the altars of Baal and preparing for his impending battle with the Midianites, Gideon again asked God for another sign that he had been called by God.

> Then Gideon said to God, "If you will save Israel by my hand, as you have said, behold, I am laying a fleece of wool on the threshing floor. If there is dew on the fleece alone, and it is dry on all the ground, then I shall

> know that you will save Israel by my hand, as you have said." And it was so. When he rose early next morning and squeezed the fleece, he wrung enough dew from the fleece to fill a bowl with water. (Judges 6:36–38)

Still needing further proof, Gideon asked God to keep the fleece dry while the ground around it was wet with dew. With this proof, his assurance that God would use him to deliver Israel, Gideon was strengthened.

Gideon was so unsure of himself. Do you ever read his story and think, *How much proof do you need?* Gideon needed proof that God was assigning him the task, that he was the right man for the job, and also that God's presence was with him. So often, we are no different from Gideon. We need more proof. So what did Gideon do? He sought God, asked to see Him, and received God's assurances.

Perhaps God has assigned you a task you feel you just cannot handle. You know what He is asking, but you are just not sure you have the resources, ability, or wisdom to accomplish it. Maybe you aren't even sure He is asking. Things seem so unclear, and you are not sure what to do. You need further proof it is God directing you as well as more instruction on the required task. As you take it before the Lord in prayer and seek advice from godly friends, trust God's assurances when He continues to guide you toward His plan. Know that God does not give you a job He hasn't first prepared you for. God equips you with all you need to accomplish all He has called you to do. He will be with you and give you grace and strength for each moment. Because this is His promise, you can trust His help to accomplish your task.

In what ways do you feel inadequate for a task God has called you to do?

How have you asked God to show proof He is there?

_____

_____

_____

_____

*Proof of being called is reaching out in faith to the hand
that is reaching out to lead you.*

CALLED WITH ASSURANCE

Then the Lord said to him,
"Who has made man's mouth?
Who makes him mute, or deaf, or seeing, or blind?
Is it not I, the Lord?"

EXODUS 4:11

Through many generations, believers have sung the beloved hymn "There Is a Fountain Filled with Blood," a reminder of Christ's death wiping away the stain of sin. The songwriter, William Cowper, wrote this hymn in 1772 after working through a bout of depression. He had battled through struggles of severe depression and attempts at suicide for much of his life, but God had a plan. During Cowper's time in an asylum in 1763, Dr. Nathaniel Cotton purposefully left a Bible on a bench for Cowper to find. Through time in God's Word, Cowper accepted the Lord as his Savior, opening his heart as a vessel for God's use.

Cowper's true talent was found in writing. He was known internationally for poetry, but he was a recluse who spent virtually all his adult life in the rural English countryside. Though his mental struggles continued, God's indwelling Spirit influenced the works he penned.

In 1765, John Newton became Cowper's pastor, counselor, and friend. Newton was a constant encouragement and assured Cowper of

God's work in his life. He drew Cowper into ministry, and together they wrote a book of hymns. Through his beautifully written poetry and hymns, God used Cowper to touch the hearts of people.

Like William Cowper, Moses needed assurance God could use his words. God called to Moses out of a burning bush one day. He placed the call on Moses, and Moses responded with the question "Who am I?" (Exodus 3:11). The conversation continued with proof of who God was and signs of His power, but the real issue was assurance. Moses lacked confidence in his ability to speak. He did not feel he could do what God was asking him to do. God's response showed him he could. "Then the Lord said to him, 'Who has made man's mouth? Who makes him mute, or deaf, or seeing, or blind? Is it not I, the Lord? Now therefore go, and I will be with your mouth and teach you what you shall speak'" (Exodus 4:11–12).

God formed Moses for a purpose. God knew the ways Moses felt he was weak, but He wanted to use Moses's perceived weaknesses for His glory. Moses was thinking too much about himself and how he would look rather than the work God was calling him to do. Using Moses as His vessel, God would do the work. It was up to Moses to trust God and deliver the message.

God created us with gifts and abilities. He uniquely created us to use those gifts to accomplish different tasks throughout our lives. God knew from the beginning how He would use each of us, so He made sure we had all we needed. The problem is, we are unsure of our gifts and abilities. We see weakness, but God sees strength as we look to Him to use those weaknesses for His glory. So often we feel we aren't equipped. Our efforts will end in failure. We don't have what it takes. Like Moses, we are afraid. Fear should cause us to turn to God for help, where we will receive needed confidence in ourselves as God's creation.

When God calls you to do a task, He gives you everything you need to fulfill His purposes. All God needs is your willingness to be used as the beautifully created vessel He made you. God uses each of you. It may not be through your words like Moses or William Cowper, but He has given you your own gifts. With a willing heart and His presence in the work assigned, He will use those gifts so others might see Him. You can have confidence in your gifts and abilities because you know the One who gifts them to you.

What are some weaknesses you see in yourself?
How do you use them as an excuse for not doing what God calls you to do?
Do you remember who made you?

_____
_____
_____

Confidence comes in knowing the Giver knows how to use the gifts you have.

CALLED TO PLANT SEEDS

*I planted, Apollos watered, but God gave the growth.
So neither he who plants nor he who waters is
anything, but only God who gives the growth.*

1 CORINTHIANS 3:6–7

Quietness filling the meeting room is suddenly broken by loud grumbling. In growing embarrassment, you realize your stomach has let everyone know lunchtime is near. Sometimes hunger causes lightheadedness or weakness, a feeling of being completely famished. We have all experienced these feelings but know that relief comes with a good meal. What if it were your last meal? Could relief come if no more food were available? What would it be like to know you were facing starvation? Most of us will never experience anything like that in our world with plenty or at least enough.

Even Elijah didn't experience this fear. In 1 Kings 17, God sent him to boldly announce to King Ahab that He was sending a drought. The people of Israel had turned their hearts to idols rather than serving Him. They prayed to Baal, the god of fertility, to provide water needed for their crops rather than the God who is over all creation. Since Elijah was in danger because of the king's reaction, God led him to a brook and commanded ravens to bring him food. Through the effects of the drought, the brook dried up. God sent Elijah to be aided by a widow in Zarephath, a city of Sidon, a Gentile territory outside Israel.

This widow knew the fear of starvation. The drought had affected the region in which she lived. Daily the widow watched her flour and oil. Frantically she stretched it, trying to make it last as long as possible not just for herself; no, she had a precious son to feed. Finally came the day when all that was left was enough for one last meal. Despair filled her heart as she gathered sticks to prepare this meal for herself and her son before starvation took hold.

But despair changed to surprise through a simple request. "And he (Elijah) called to her and said, 'Bring me a little water in a vessel, that I may drink.' And as she was going to bring it, he called to her and said, 'Bring me a morsel of bread in your hand'" (1 Kings 17:10–11). Not only that, on hearing of her situation, Elijah responded in a way that stunned her. "And Elijah said to her, 'Do not fear; go and do as you have said. But first make me a little cake of it and bring it to me, and afterward make something for yourself and your son.'" (v. 13).

Had she heard him right? Elijah had asked her to take a step of faith and feed him first. What dread she had faced in previous days watching her flour and oil dwindle, yet she was asked to give all that she had. She was not even being asked to eat the last meal with Elijah and believe God would provide; Elijah asked her to take *all* she had to make his meal and *then* make a meal for herself and her son. Elijah promised if she trusted his God, He would supply, and she would have all she needed until the drought was over. Elijah in his call to trust was really asking her to trust in His God.

She must have sensed from the beginning that Elijah served the true living God. In her response to his request, she began "As the Lord your God lives" (v. 12). Something in Elijah caused her to trust. She didn't hesitate. "And she went and did as Elijah said" (1 Kings 17:15). A seed of faith in God had sprouted.

From then on, going over to her flour barrel and oil jar every day, she had just enough bread to bake for one more day. The widow of Zarephath gave even when she had nothing left to give. Day after day she saw her needs met as God provided. Before, she had been preparing her final meal—then God. Her journey of faith sprouted when the aid given to Elijah actually became the aid she needed to see God. God can use one moment of trust to build and strengthen the foundation of trust for the next moment.

Faith is like that. Faith is a firm belief in the absence of proof. God often asks us to take these steps of faith because He knows what those steps will produce in those around us. The strength of our faith may cause people crossing our path to take a step leading to Him. Your involvement with people around you, even asking for their help, may be just the help they need to see God.

How is God calling you to step out in faith?
What are ways you can begin to interact with those around you to help their faith sprout?
Have you seen moments of trust in your life that have strengthened your foundation of trust in God?

_____

_____

_____

_____

A step of faith leads to a life of faithfulness.

CALLED TO LIFE ETERNAL

And the woman said to Elijah, "Now I know that you are a man of God, and that the word of the Lord in your mouth is truth."

1 KINGS 17:24

As soon as the calendar indicates spring is near, I watch the outdoors for signs of life. Walking through the woods, I look for buds beginning to form on branches and tiny sprouts poking through the dirt. Days go on, and I continue to watch as buds form flowers and sprouts turn into stems. Weeks pass, and flowers with leaves fill the trees. Stems have strengthened to support tulips, daffodils, and hyacinths. Growth unseen becomes the beauty we see and enjoy.

Spring was coming to the widow of Zarephath. In the same way I watch the developing spring, Elijah watched spring developing in her heart.

Elijah's faith ignited hope in this woman, but hope was dashed as her beloved son became ill. The severity of his illness brought his death. How could this be? Anguish overwhelmed her heart as she cried out in grief to Elijah, "What have you against me, O man of God? You have come to me to bring my sin to remembrance and to cause the death of my son!" (1 Kings 17:18).

Her thinking distraught, the widow felt God's attention was on her home and her sins, and now this God had taken from her what mattered most, her son. She felt condemned by Elijah's holy God. However, in her grief and struggling trust, she could not see that this God of justice was also a God who longed to extend His love and grace to her. In her small faith, she could not see this great God.

Elijah could. He knew his God. Hearing her grief-filled accusations, he did not falter but took the child and immediately went to the One who was the foundation for his life. A simple phrase guided his life: "before whom I stand" (1 Kings 17:1). Often in proclaiming God's message, Elijah would encounter hostility and utter this phrase. However, this phrase was more than simple. It was a proclamation that he served the living God. God's power alone gave him the inner strength, wisdom, and power to do all that God called him to do. Speaking this expression in moments of strain and difficulty clearly showed the godly strength that came from the depths of his heart. At this moment, Elijah knew he needed to go to his strength. He went to God.

Taking the child before the Lord in his upper chamber, Elijah prayed, stretching himself three times upon the child.

> And the Lord listened to the voice of Elijah. And the life of the child came into him again, and he revived. And Elijah took the child and brought him down from the upper chamber into the house and delivered him to his mother. And Elijah said, "See, your son lives."
> (1 Kings 17:22–23)

"See, your son lives." A simple sentence Elijah used to point the woman to God. He wanted her to see what God had done, how God had brought life back to her son, and how God offered her life. Eternal life was hers if she would accept the love, grace, and forgiveness that the God of Israel was extending to her, this Gentile widow from Zarephath. Her confession of faith comes, and she trusts God as her own. The widow of Zarephath came to Elijah's aid when, in reality, God used him to give aid to her spiritual darkness.

Sometimes in our lives, we are called to trust God when we don't understand why. Elijah couldn't understand why God would take the life of this child, but he was called to trust God's plan. You see, the woman was called by God to have faith in Him. He graciously extended His gift of salvation to her, but she needed to see Him in more than just providing her daily bread. The provision of her needs by God caused her faith to sprout, but the life restored to her son by God gave her confirmation that Elijah's God was the one true God, and she took Him as her own.

You may feel God calling you to perform a task or reach out to someone when it doesn't make sense. You have no understanding of why God would ask you to do this or how you could make a difference to this person. Although we cannot see His plan, God knows the small act or word that will cause a person to move forward toward their faith in Him. Your obedience to God's plan may bring a person from a small spark of faith to an overwhelming trust in the Savior.

*How have you heard God calling you?
When He leads you along a path or toward a situation you don't understand, what is your response?*

_____
_____
_____
_____

*"Before whom I stand" gives all the strength needed
to answer His call.*

CALLED TO SAVE

And he said, "Abba, Father, all things are possible for you. Remove this cup from me. Yet not what I will, but what you will."

MARK 14:36

The *Webster's* definition for *calling* is "a strong inner impulse toward a particular course of action especially when accompanied by conviction of divine influence."[5] Wow—quite the definition. Have you ever felt called, like God was leading you toward a task or a ministry? Some are called to be pastors. People are called to a mission field. Believers can feel called to minister to individuals. Jesus was called. His was perhaps the greatest calling God ever gave. Jesus was called to give His life that all mankind might live.

Nothing about Jesus's calling to earth was easy. In coming to earth as a human baby, He gave up His divine attributes to become one of us. He was still fully God, but He was also fully man. He came to earth as a baby. Luke tells us, "Jesus increased in wisdom and in stature and in favor with God and man" (Luke 2:52). Jesus, being truly human, grew up as any child would. He did not understand His unique relationship

---

5 "Calling." *Merriam-Webster.com Dictionary*, Merriam-Webster. https://www.merriam-webster.com/dictionary/calling. Accessed 4 Dec. 2023.

with the Father right away. He had to go through the same learning and maturing process as every other person. He relied on God. He spent large amounts of time talking to His Father and seeking His will. He knew He needed God and trusted in God and His plan.

Jesus understands hurts and struggles. He knows God calls us to do some difficult things. While He lived His life here on earth, He experienced many of the difficulties and struggles we do. Though Jesus knew His purpose in coming to this earth was to fulfill God's divine plan, He struggled to do the Father's will.

> And he said to them, "My soul is very sorrowful, even to death. Remain here and watch." And going a little farther, he fell on the ground and prayed that, if it were possible, the hour might pass from him. And he said, "Abba, Father, all things are possible for you. Remove this cup from me. Yet not what I will, but what you will." (Mark 14:34–36)

Jesus knew what was coming, and He knew there would be a time when He would be alienated from His Father. It was almost more than He could bear. He asked if God's redemptive purposes could still be achieved without His sacrifice on the cross. He was not asking God to go back on His promises. He just asked if it could be achieved in another way.

This was not a sign of weakness in Jesus but rather His knowledge of the agony He would experience in His holiness as He bore the weight of the sin of all mankind. Knowing the suffering that was about to take place took Him to a deeper anguish than we have ever known. What did He do? He went to His Father. His purpose in prayer was not to change

God's mind. Rather, His purpose was to align His desires and will with God's. Jesus willingly placed His desires in submission to His Father's will.

The calling placed on Jesus was greater than any calling ever placed on anyone else. Jesus was called to leave the presence of His Father and set aside His divine attributes to become human. He alone experienced something we never will. He was separated from His Father; nothing can ever separate us from God. In having the sins of all mankind laid on Him, He endured the separation that led to our salvation. Jesus fulfilled God's calling to save. His call to us is a call to trust in Him and the work He did on the cross.

You may be called by God to minister for Him in a specific task or ministry. Even if what He is asking is not easy, you can be assured He will be with you. Jesus gave a call to every believer before returning to His Father in heaven after He fulfilled His own call: "Go therefore and make disciples of all nations, baptizing them in the name of the Father and of the Son and of the Holy Spirit, teaching them to observe all that I have commanded you. And behold, I am with you always, to the end of the age" (Matthew 28:19–20). You are called to share the purpose of His call with those around you, and even in this great call, Jesus has promised to be with you. However, the greatest call He has given you is to accept His precious gift of salvation for yourself. Have you accepted this call?

What calling is God asking you to fulfill?
How are you struggling with the call He has on your life?
_____
_____
_____
_____

*In calling us, God offers Himself to enable us
to do what He has called us to do.*

TRUST WHEN YOU DON'T UNDERSTAND

Dear Lord, I just don't get it. The situation was already hard, but now this? Why did You allow it? How will this even help? I wish I could understand, and I keep trying to, but I simply can't. How will this lead to good? My emotions spin out of control as I try to gain understanding of Your plan. I grab ahold of Your promises, maybe not understanding, but with assurance that You will be with me in every moment.

WHAT IS AN ARK?

For I know the plans I have for you, declares the Lord, plans for welfare and not for evil, to give you a future and a hope.

JEREMIAH 29:11

Gentle breezes lift tendrils of hair tickling a face. Leaves caught in a whirlwind of auburn, reds, and yellows gather in the crook of a tree. With a resounding boom, a towering tree uproots as it falls to the ground.

Wind cannot be seen, but no mind can doubt its existence. We trust the wind is there because we see the results of what it can do. As we live a life of faith, often we must trust God in what we do not see, like wind. However, Noah was given a look at what was unseen.

> And God said to Noah, "I have determined to make an end of all flesh, for the earth is filled with violence through them. Behold, I will destroy them with the earth. Make yourself an ark of gopher wood. Make rooms in the ark, and cover it inside and out with pitch … For behold, I will bring a flood of waters upon the earth to destroy all flesh in which is the breath of life under heaven. Everything that is on the earth shall die.

> But I will establish my covenant with you, and you shall come into the ark, you, your sons, your wife, and your sons' wives with you." (Genesis 6:13–14; 17–18)

God let Noah know in advance what He was going to do and told Noah how to prepare for it. What took much faith was that there had never been a flood on the earth. Noah did not know what rain was, let alone an ark. At that time, water did not fall from the sky but came up from the ground, and no one had ever seen an ark. Noah and his sons followed God's instructions and built this place of safety in the midst of ridicule. He held on to his faith in God that all God said would come to pass. His righteousness saved him and his family as he stepped aboard the ark. The rest of the world was destroyed because of their lack of faith in God.

Sometimes God lets us in on His plan. He so clearly directs us. We know exactly what He wants us to do and how He wants us to go about it. However, sometimes even when we know that, nothing makes sense. We have no understanding of why He is asking us to do things a certain way. Things are not the way we think they should be or the way others expect them to be. If you are following God's direction, however, things are exactly as they are supposed to be. Even when things do not make sense to us and we have no understanding, if we are following God's plan, it is good, and we can trust it is for our good.

> For I know the plans I have for you, declares the Lord, plans for welfare and not for evil, to give you a future and a hope. Then you will call upon me and come and pray to me, and I will hear you. You will seek me and find me, when you seek me with all your heart.
> (Jeremiah 29:11–13)

God has not asked us to figure out His plan. He knows what it is and how He wants to take us there. We may not know what it looks like, and things may end up different from what people expect or how we think it should be. So many whys may never be answered, but we do have all the answers needed as we trust God. He will show us exactly how to carry out His purposes.

Have you ever been so sure of God's plan, but the steps to accomplish that plan just do not make sense? Like the wind, you have to trust what you do not see. Remember that God does see. He knows His plan and what He needs you to do for all to come out perfectly. When you seek Him with all your heart, you will find Him. He will lead you toward a future for your good and His glory, even when what you see does not make sense.

How have God's requests of you been hard to understand?
What do you do when things turn out far differently from how you expect?
How do you respond to others when God's plan doesn't lead to what they expect from you?

_____

_____

_____

_____

Don't look for an answer to the whys;
instead ask, Why not?

WHAT'S THE PLAN?

*Trust in the Lord with all your heart,
and do not lean on your own understanding.*

PROVERBS 3:5

David Brainerd had a plan. Don't we often have a plan? We know the path we want to take based on our likes and dislikes, the way God is leading us. In obedience we move forward on what we feel is God's call for our lives. David Brainerd made a commitment to God to enter into ministry before he even knew the Lord as his Savior! He had a plan.

David experienced God's grace and entered into a saving relationship with God at the age of twenty-one. He enrolled at Yale and began to prepare for the ministry. Becoming seriously ill with tuberculosis, he was sent home in his second year. David was able to return to Yale, but his time there was short as he was expelled in his third year. David had pointed out the carnality and hypocrisy of some faculty by making uncharitable comments during a time when students experienced a spiritual awakening. His dreams and obedience to God's call suddenly were destroyed as he was asked to leave. At that time, only a degree from Yale, Harvard, or a European university would lead to becoming an established minister in Connecticut. David's plan ended when his circumstances changed. However, this was all a part of God's plan for him.

In writing the book of Proverbs, Solomon reminded us of the wisdom of trusting God's plan. "Trust in the Lord with all your heart, and do not lean on your own understanding. In all your ways acknowledge him, and he will make straight your paths" (Proverbs 3:5–6). The godly wisdom in these verses is so basic and easy to understand but so hard to follow when we can't understand and when everything changes. But that's what God asks us to do.

In the summer of 1742, David Brainerd was approached by a group of ministers from New Lights who licensed him to preach and suggested he become a missionary to the Indians. He had the opportunity to minister to many different tribes in the United States and lead many Native Americans to the Lord.

What makes Brainerd's testimony so powerful is the fact that he followed God obediently in missionary work while in the midst of suffering. Brainerd shared the gospel when he was weak and suffering from tuberculosis, discouraged, beaten down, and often lonely. The severity of his suffering was incredible, yet he continued in his work. He let the Lord direct his path.

Before succumbing to the disease at the age of twenty-nine, Brainerd expressed his heart. "All my desire was the conversion of the heathen, and all my hope was in God: God does not suffer me to please or comfort myself with hopes of seeing friends, returning to my dear acquaintance, and enjoying worldly comforts."[6]

Brainerd's life seems tragic. He died so young while being used greatly by God with the Native American peoples. Even in his darkest times, he could still affirm the truth and goodness of God. His life was

---

6   John Piper, *Tested By Fire: The Fruit of Suffering in the Lives of John Bunyan, William Cowper, and David Brainerd* (Westmont, Illinois: InterVarsity Press, 2001), 145.

a testimony of perseverance through suffering, which continues to be an inspiration and encouragement to missionaries even today through his biography recorded by Jonathan Edwards.

Sometimes you have to make a firm choice to trust. When you are in the middle of deep heartache and you don't want to move forward or do it anymore or when everything changes, what is it going to be: doubt God's goodness, or trust Him because He has never stopped being a good God? Circumstances don't change God. He never changes. How we view circumstances changes how we see God.

We need to see God through the lens of His truth. We need to always remember we have a never-changing God in complete control of both ever-changing and never-changing circumstances. When His plan becomes your plan, you follow God obediently regardless of where that plan takes you.

What is your plan?
How has God's plan differed from your plan?
What steps are you taking to set aside understanding and just follow Him?

_____

_____

_____

_____

> *Entrusting our lives to God's will allows us to rise out of anxieties and fears, the unknown and the hard to understand, and peacefully follow the plan God is working out for us.*

WHY ARE YOU CAST DOWN?

Why are you cast down, O my soul, and why are you in turmoil within me? Hope in God; for I shall again praise him, my salvation and my God.

PSALM 42:5

Emotions are crazy. Sometimes they pop up out of nowhere. A song, an object, a word, a memory can cause tears to form as you remember grief due to the loss of a loved one or the loss of a dream. Those same things can cause laughter and joy as you remember. Emotions come out at different times in different ways. They can be hard to understand, but they should not control us. I am realizing more and more that having emotions doesn't indicate a lack of trust. It is a part of what makes us human. When emotions control us and keep us from trusting God, keep us in the same place instead of moving forward in growth, there is then an indication of a problem.

The book of Psalms is filled with emotion, which is why so many relate and receive comfort from its verses.

> Why are you cast down, O my soul, and why are you in turmoil within me? (Psalm 42:5)
>
> How long, O Lord? Will you forget me forever? How long will you hide your face from me? How long must I

> take counsel in my soul and have sorrow in my heart all the day? How long shall my enemy be exalted over me? (Psalm 13:1–2)

> Come and hear, all you who fear God, and I will tell what he has done for my soul. I cried to him with my mouth, and high praise was on my tongue. (Psalm 66:16–17)

In this selection of psalms, different emotions are expressed by these men. We need emotions. They show life. They are indicators of what is going on in our hearts. Sometimes though, emotions will get out of balance, causing us to doubt, question, or quit trusting in God.

Our God is an emotional God. But unlike us, He will always think, feel, and react in ways that are consistent with who He is. His unchanging nature makes it impossible for Him to respond emotionally in a way that goes against His divine nature. He understands our emotions and the differences between His and ours. When our emotions take over and cause us to doubt, when we can't understand why we feel the way we do, God has provided His Comforter to help us see truth through our emotions and trust again.

The Spirit of God is capable of bringing our emotions back under control as we allow His emotions to become ours. When life causes emotional upheaval, the emotions we experience will be His as we allow His presence in our hearts to change us. He will help us test our emotions as we think through "whatever is true, whatever is honorable, whatever is just, whatever is pure, whatever is lovely, whatever is commendable, if there is any excellence, if there is anything worthy of praise" (Philippians 4:8). We may not understand our circumstances, but our emotional response to them will keep us trusting in Him as we respond as God would.

Recognize your emotions, but don't stay in them. Don't ignore them but instead make sure that what is causing your emotions, especially if hard, is fully given to the Lord. As you trust God with your circumstances—good and bad—your emotions should come back to a good balance so you can move forward for Him.

After expressing their emotions, so many writers of the psalms came to the following conclusions:

> Wait for the Lord; be strong, and let your heart take courage; wait for the Lord! (Psalm 27:14)

> Be strong, and let your heart take courage, all you who wait for the Lord! (Psalm 31:24)

> Hope in God; for I shall again praise him, my salvation and my God. (Psalm 42:5)

How are your emotions controlling you?
How are they keeping you from trusting God?

_____

_____

_____

_____

Just a song caused memories to flood back of a walk alone, an unfulfilled dream. Tears of sadness led to the choice to trust God's sovereign plan.

HOW CAN THIS BE GOOD?

You keep him in perfect peace whose mind is stayed on you, because he trusts in you.

ISAIAH 26:3

How can I describe my dear friend Kathy? Full of fun and life, a beautiful redhead, Kathy dedicates her days to teaching students math. She is one of those teachers who knows how to teach and has a love for her students. Kathy grew up the youngest of four children in a pastor's home. Her foundation was built very early on the Lord. Her faith is solid. She married a wonderful man, and they have a lovely daughter. Kathy loves the water, with her favorite spot being Chautauqua Lake in New York. She loves vacationing with her family and friends. She loves ministering, especially to teens and young marrieds. She is very organized, very type A.

To look at her, you would never know that Kathy was born with a bad heart valve and underwent three heart surgeries during her sixty years of life. That isn't what took her, though. For the last three years of her life, Kathy battled with myeloma (blood/bone marrow cancer). Kathy did not wish for all these physical problems to define her. What defined Kathy all her life was Christ and her relationship with Him.

Kathy lived a life of faith; however, this did not mean she did not struggle in her walk. Her cancer walk was incredibly hard as she underwent a stem-cell transplant that did not work. She went through several different rounds of chemo that were ineffective in stopping the cancer. All along the way, she experienced ups and downs as she battled side effects. Her case caused difficulty from the start with her heart issues and being on blood thinner. Doctors constantly watched and adjusted procedures as her body reacted to different treatments. One of her favorite verses was Philippians 4:13: "I can do all things through him who strengthens me." She believed this and trusted that regardless of what she would next face, she could face it because she trusted God.

Paul wrote, "And we know that for those who love God all things work together for good, for those who are called according to his purpose" (Romans 8:28). How could anything Kathy faced be good? She suffered so much through the course of her life. Cancer was the most difficult. She once told me that she could handle all the heart surgeries. She knew what to expect. Cancer was constantly throwing curveballs at her; so many unexpected symptoms and difficulties would suddenly take place, causing the doctors to reevaluate and restrategize her treatment. Her life was hard to understand.

Still, even in the questioning, the low times, the times of despair, Kathy held on to her trust in God. Her foundation remained firm. Life seemed hard to understand, and the suffering seemed unfair, but God—His plan is perfect. His ways are good, for her good. She didn't have to understand, she just had to trust. She held on to the words of Isaiah 26:3: "You keep him in perfect peace whose mind is stayed on you, because he trusts in you."

God doesn't call us to understand. He doesn't promise us a good life. He promises that all we face in life will work for good, and He promises His strength and grace to go through each moment. We are never without His help. Kathy lived a life of courage and faith. She might have lost her battle with cancer, but she lived a life of victory with her God, who was faithful in every aspect of her life.

I had the privilege of helping to care for some of her needs and spent time with her at the hospital. I will treasure those times, but what I will treasure most is the godly example of the trust Kathy clearly showed as she faced incredibly difficult circumstances that she simply couldn't understand.

What circumstances cause you to seek answers from God? How do you build your trust in God to face what you don't understand?

_____

_____

_____

_____

Peace doesn't come by understanding.
Peace comes by trusting in the One who understands.

WHAT TRUST DOES FOR YOU

Gracious Lord, I am beginning to see now! My small steps of trust in You build to greater heights of trust. Obediently following Your ways prepares me for the next steps of faith You ask me to take. As I cling to You and move forward in my journey, joy comes even when the journey remains hard. I know without a doubt that if all else fails, You will never fail, and because of this, I can trust You with every moment.

AN UNDIVIDED HEART

*Teach me your way, O Lord, that I may walk
in your truth; unite my heart to fear your name.*

PSALM 86:11

Have you ever been troubled, struggled with a temptation, held onto a worry, or just needed to know the way? Often these are thoughts that keep me up in the night. I will pray, earnestly seeking help from the Lord to show me and direct me, to speak to me from His Word. I should not be surprised anymore when the very next morning I am receiving His answers in an abundance of ways. I feel like His answers end up being my theme for the week as I see Him showing me the same verses in a devotion, paragraphs in a book I am reading, teaching from a sermon, or thoughts brought up in conversation with a friend. When I ask Him to show or direct my steps, He always will.

David also asked the Lord to teach him and show him the way so that he would have an undivided heart to follow God. "Teach me your way, Lord, that I may rely on your faithfulness; give me an undivided heart, that I may fear your name. I will praise you, Lord my God, with all my heart; I will glorify your name forever" (Psalm 86:11–12 NIV).

David did not want to pursue two conflicting ways to live. He knew that following God with single-minded devotion would lead to obedience and worship. God would receive the glory for the work done in his life as David would point people to God through how he lived.

Those who truly belong to God show that relationship by how they live. A person cannot be devoted to two masters: "No one can serve two masters, for either he will hate the one and love the other, or he will be devoted to the one and despise the other. You cannot serve God and money" (Matthew 6:24).

God alone is worthy of being served with our complete and absolute devotion, the simple reason being that He is God. When our heart is divided, we are weak because we are seeking something or someone other than God. We are placing people or things above God. We say we are devoted to God but place our security and faith in people, circumstances, or things. Our heart is divided, causing confusion along our path. We struggle to know where to place our trust, and our foundation crumbles.

Only when our hearts are fully fixed on God are we strong. Our foundation is firm, and the journey God takes us on can be trusted because He can be trusted. God's desire for His children is to live a life of abundance, which comes by submitting our will to His will. Our responsibility is to voluntarily walk according to His leading. He is our trusted friend and helper as He guides us along our appointed path. He sees our beginning and our end, leading us in between to a life that will be abundant and bring Him glory if we just follow Him in faith.

As you learn of God's character and ways through the Bible, see Him at work in your life, and follow His guidance, you learn to trust Him more. You rely on His faithfulness, knowing He is trustworthy. Your faith will grow as your understanding of Him grows. Your response will become devotion to God alone. God will be your only master.

Ask and He will answer, maybe through a quiet thought, a word from a friend, or a verse. God works through His Holy Spirit transforming hearts and minds to make them undivided.

Where do you see areas where you are not wholly devoted to God?
What do you need to give up for God to be your only master?
Are you willing to walk according to His leading?

_____

_____

_____

_____

An undivided heart invites a faithful God
to bring you to a place of obedience and worship.

COURAGE UNDER FIRE

*Fear not, for I am with you; be not dismayed,
for I am your God; I will strengthen you,
I will help you, I will uphold you
with my righteous right hand.*

ISAIAH 41:10

The Congressional Medal of Honor is a US military decoration awarded for valor or courage in combat. Suspended from a blue ribbon, the medal has a center pad containing thirteen white stars and represents courage under fire. Drawing on courage, soldiers found the mental strength to do what they had to do on the battlefield.

Daily life calls many to draw on inner strength to venture, persevere, and withstand danger, fear, or difficulty. It takes courage to walk beside a wayward child. It takes courage to stay in a failing marriage. It takes courage to minister God's truth to unreceptive hearts. Any situation God asks you to move forward in with continuous pain and difficulty takes courage.

Daniel 6 records the success of Daniel, an Israelite brought with others in captivity to Babylon. Daniel quickly gained favor with King Darius. The goal of the king was to place Daniel over all the satraps and the high officials so that they would all report to Daniel. This did not sit well with these officials, and they immediately began to think of a plot to take Daniel out of this position. They persuaded the king to sign a law commanding all to bow down to him alone or be cast into the den of lions. Of course, this sounded good to the king. Who wouldn't want to be honored above all else?

Daniel knew, though, only one could receive his honor and worship: the one true God. "When Daniel knew that the document had been signed, he went to his house where he had windows in his upper chamber open toward Jerusalem. He got down on his knees three times a day and prayed and gave thanks before his God, as he had done previously" (Daniel 6:10).

The officials took no time at all to report Daniel's actions to the king. They knew they had him, and soon the king knew his grave error. He truly cared for Daniel. Working all day to revoke the law, King Darius found even as king, he could not change his own ordinance. With a heavy heart, "the king commanded, and Daniel was brought and cast into the den of lions. The king declared to Daniel, 'May your God, whom you serve continually, deliver you!'" (Daniel 6:16).

After a sleepless night, King Darius rushed to the den the next morning, calling out to Daniel. Joy erupted from his heart as he heard Daniel's voice! Daniel's God had saved him from the mouths of the lions. After dealing with the evil officials, King Darius made a decree for his people to fear the one true God, describing Him as "the living God, enduring forever … He delivers and rescues; he works signs and wonders in heaven and on earth, he who has saved Daniel from the power of the lions" (Daniel 6:26-27).

Because of the eagerness of the evil officials to remove Daniel from his position, he quickly had to draw upon courage to carry him through this unfair decree. Daniel did not hesitate to continue his relationship and worship of the Father, because he trusted God. The strength of Daniel's trust in God had been built upon time after time of God strengthening him, helping him, and upholding him as he faced a lifetime of trials. Daniel's life was a testimony of courage and trust, and because he remained faithful to God, an entire nation saw God's glory and power through Daniel's deliverance from the lions.

To follow God's leading and trust Him takes courage when you can't see the path and the hope you hold on to is just a speck. But because you trust God, you can have courage to continue the course. You can trust that God has you where you are supposed to be. You can hold on to the smallest speck of hope, knowing God is in control and is able to change any unending pain. He promises grace and strength for each moment and has made you an heir of eternal hope. The pain will not last forever, and He will never leave you alone in it. With obedient trust will flow peace and joy, even when the grief and pain of the situation continue year after year.

How is God asking you to persevere and withstand in the face of difficulty?
What situations in the past helped to build your trust in Him?

_____

_____

_____

_____

Courage is quiet, unfailing trust in God, who carries you through unending difficulty.

A LIFE OF REJOICING

Yet I will rejoice in the Lord;
I will take joy in the God of my salvation.

HABAKKUK 3:18

Charles Lane Martin was born on November 11, 2015. Even before he was five years old, Charlie was known for his sweet smile lighting up an entire room, his big, beautiful eyes melting hearts, and his ability to bring joy to everyone. Charlie loved to wear bow ties, read and learn, attend school parties, nap with his mom, chat with his dad at the end of a long day, and snuggle with those he loved. Charlie lived a life of bravery and endurance. He was a patient teacher to his parents, family, and friends. Yes, Charlie was a teacher to those who gave him his special care—really, to anyone who knew Charlie.

Born with rhizomelic chondrodysplasia punctata (RCDP), Charlie was a "rhizo" kid. He was a little person who needed constant help through breathing treatments, feeds, physical therapy, and medications for seizures, pain, reflux, congestion, and appetite enhancers. He loved to attend school, but he taught as much as he learned. Charlie taught each person touched by his life about love, courage, resilience, and patience. He taught those around him that each day is special, each person is made for a purpose, and joy can be found in the midst of hardship. Though

Charlie experienced pain and suffering and was never able to run and jump like other boys his age, he lived a life of joy.

The prophet Habakkuk watched the people of Judah turn from God and endure much suffering. He struggled to understand how God could let this nation continue in their evil ways, and he did not understand God and His silence as the wickedness thrived. How long would God let this continue? When God did reveal His plan to use the wicked nation of Babylon to punish Judah, Habakkuk again questioned God. How could God use a nation more wicked than Judah to punish His own people? Although Habakkuk never came to a full understanding of God's ways, he did come to a place of surrender as he learned to completely rely on God's wisdom and justice. We witness Habakkuk's struggle turn to trust in his sovereign, unfailing God:

> Though the fig tree should not blossom, nor fruit be on the vines, the produce of the olive fail and the fields yield no food, the flock be cut off from the fold and there be no herd in the stalls, yet I will rejoice in the Lord; I will take joy in the God of my salvation. (Habakkuk 3:17–18)

When Chris and Chelsey, Charlie's parents, learned that their son would be born with RCDP, they struggled and questioned God's plan. How could God allow this to happen? But only for a moment. Chris and Chelsey trusted in a sovereign God. Through past difficulties, they both fully knew and believed that we do not always see and understand how God's plan is unfolding. They chose to place their trust and hope in knowing God was working. They rejoiced in seeing the blessing that arose out of the pain as God used Charlie to touch so many hearts. He

A LIFE OF REJOICING

made all things beautiful through Charlie's life. Because God was their life, Chris and Chelsey could cling to Him and trust His plan, knowing Charlie's life was full of purpose. They could rejoice because they knew God was at work in ways they could not see.

Charlie Martin lost his battle with RCDP on April 28, 2021. Yes, he went to the arms of Jesus free from pain and suffering, but his life is not remembered because of suffering at the hands of RCDP. Charlie's life was full of joy and happiness. His testimony continues to impact people, reminding them to make the most of each day, to find joy in the small things, and that through it all, it is well because of Jesus.

When you cling to God and allow Him to be your life, you will not falter when all is taken away because nothing can take God away from you. Because of that assurance, you can rejoice.

What joy can you see in your painful situation?
What steps can you take in trusting God when all seems lost?

_____

_____

_____

Rejoicing through pain comes through trust
in our sovereign, unfailing God.

JOY IN OBEDIENCE

*Commit your way to the Lord; trust in him,
and he will act.*

PSALM 37:5

"Laura" is a friend I met long ago. Her story is still her reality, so with permission, I can share her story but not her real name. Married after college, she was on the path to having her only true dream in life fulfilled—a happy marriage and a large family. However, not many years into her marriage, she found her dreams and reality far different. Expectations from those closest to her ran high, and she felt less than important. She couldn't do anything right. She couldn't live up to the standards. She was not seen as the person God created her to be. She was never enough. Soon, she started to believe this and lost herself. Though she knew the Lord, she no longer knew who she was as His child.

Years went by, circumstances did not change, and when given the choice, Laura chose to be obedient to God and remain in a hard marriage. She knew obedience to God and trust in His plan were her journey. Though her dreams of a family came to fruition, Laura lived her life feeling lost and alone. She played her part as a good Christian should, hiding what was going on from those outside and drawing further inside herself, away from God and others. Still, because she trusted God, she obeyed.

Mark's gospel shares how the disciples' obedience to Jesus led them into great trouble.

> Immediately he made his disciples get into the boat and go before him to the other side, to Bethsaida, while he dismissed the crowd. And after he had taken leave of them, he went up on the mountain to pray ... And he saw that they were making headway painfully, for the wind was against them. And about the fourth watch of the night he came to them, walking on the sea ... they all saw him and were terrified. But immediately he spoke to them and said, "Take heart; it is I. Do not be afraid." (Mark 6:45–46, 48, 50)

After ministering and miraculously providing food for a crowd of five thousand with only five loaves of bread and two fish, Jesus needed time with His Father. He sent His disciples to Bethsaida by boat. Though He went alone on the mountain to pray, the disciples were never alone. Even on the mountain, He watched as they made their journey into the storm. He had known the difficulty coming their way, but sometimes with obedience comes difficulty. Trusting Jesus, His disciples had obeyed. Knowing the disciples' need to truly see Him, He allowed their obedience to send them into a storm.

In the early-morning hours, the disciples strained to row as the intensity of the storm increased. Jesus began His walk toward them. Doing what only He could do, He walked on the water and, for the second time that day, revealed His power and glory. For only God could walk on the water, and only God could feed five thousand people with five loaves of bread and two fish. The disciples saw the power of God right before them, but they were afraid. Jesus quietly calmed their fears as He spoke to them saying, "Take heart; it is I. Do not be afraid." Even as their obedience took a turn into the difficult and unexpected, Jesus was there. He was there for them in their obedience and called them to trust in that moment as they had trusted Him when they chose to obey.

But what would their choice be? Would they recognize Jesus as the sovereign God and trust Him in the midst of the storm, or would they stay caught in the storm? In his post "Caught in the Storm," Pastor Mark Ashley reflects on the difficulty obedience can bring.

> Obedience, the essence of trusting is like that. In the difficult and uncomfortable circumstances of life, obedience compels us to do difficult and sometimes uncomfortable things. In our minds, the path of obedience becomes more frightening than the storm itself. So we choose to remain stuck in the storm. But Jesus offers us these words of comfort in the midst of the storm, "It is I, be not afraid." And He offers to get into our boat. When we accept His offer by faith, the fierceness of the storm subsides, and He brings us to the exact place where we are supposed to be.[7]

The disciples chose to continue in the trust that had led them to obey. They brought Jesus into the boat, and the storm ceased.

In the unchanging circumstances of her life, Laura knew she had a choice. She could stay in her storm, or she could cling to God's hand as

---

7 Mark Ashley, "Caught in the Storm," (markjashley.com, October 19, 2020). https://markjashley.com/2020/10/19/caught-in-the-storm/.

He walked with her in the storm. Her search for God began, and she found Him. Freedom came as she began to see herself as God saw her. In her continuing obedience and trust, she found joy in the midst of the storm. Laura began to see her circumstances differently, and though they may never change, she had changed. The trust compelling her to obey strengthened her trust in her sovereign God. As she continues to cling to His hand in her storm, she knows she is exactly where she is supposed to be.

Where are the storms of your life taking you?
Are you still caught in your storm?
How can you invite Jesus into your boat and allow Him to navigate the storms of your life?

_____

_____

_____

_____

Joy comes in trustful obedience to the One who will walk you through the storms of life.

A TESTIMONY OF PRAISE

*He put a new song in my mouth, a song of praise
to our God. Many will see and fear,
and put their trust in the Lord.*

PSALM 40:3

Let me tell you about Jackson Dalton, a young teenager who has struggled with weight and good eating much of his life. Early in the summer, Jeff, a family friend, offered to mentor Jack as he embarked on a journey to improve his health, fitness, and confidence. They changed his diet to cleaner eating and began rigorous workouts. Jack never questioned the process but gave his all with each new obstacle. As he maintained consistency with health changes and workouts, all around him noticed his beautiful smile grew bigger and brighter. Now, Jackson holds his head high and looks people in the eye, where once he would only look toward the ground.

As I think of Jackson through this process, I am reminded of David's thoughts in Psalm 26: "Vindicate me, O Lord, for I have walked in my integrity, and I have trusted in the Lord without wavering. Prove me, O Lord, and try me; test my heart and my mind. For your steadfast love is before my eyes, and I walk in your faithfulness" (Psalm 26:1–3).

Jackson has trusted and followed the leading of Jeff, but more than that, Jeff has pointed Jackson to trusting the Lord without questioning.

He has leaned on his Lord to help him through this change of lifestyle. Jeff has not only pointed Jackson toward better health but also toward a better relationship with God. Jackson had no confidence in himself, but as he relies on the Lord and is strengthened in Him, he has a new confidence. He sees himself as God sees him, and he has been bolder in his relationship with God. His newfound confidence has enabled him to pray before adults and his peer group, where once he would have let the moment pass by. Through his story, he challenges others to do better, to set goals, and to do hard things. Jackson has become a spiritual leader.

His mom, Stephanie, explained, "He has always been sensitive to the Lord and desired to be a leader but just felt so self-defeated with his poor habits with food and lack of motion. Now he is okay with himself and knows he is trying to do better, pleases the Lord, and in turn this has allowed him to want to glorify God."

> I waited patiently for the Lord; he inclined to me and heard my cry. He drew me up from the pit of destruction, out of the miry bog, and set my feet upon a rock, making my steps secure. He put a new song in my mouth, a song of praise to our God. Many will see and fear, and put their trust in the Lord. (Psalm 40:1–3)

Jackson experienced struggle most of his life, and as David cried out for help, he also sought help. God brought the right people into his life to draw him out of his pit. The beauty of Jackson's testimony is that his change is causing others to see God.

Jackson's journey toward fitness led him to participate with his mentor, Jeff, and many others in a 5K Tough Mudder competition. Jackson completed the 5K and thirteen grueling obstacles with unwavering determination. Throughout this competition, onlookers saw beautiful acts of teamwork and selfless help offered to each competitor. It wasn't about winning but about completing. Starting out the competition with a broken finger, Jackson sustained a sprained ankle during the race. This did not stop him. He showed that though the journey may have pain, when you trust, you have security.

He trusted in others that day to help him through the difficult obstacles, but Jackson has daily trusted God to take him through the struggle of this new journey. God's journey for Jackson has put a new song in his mouth, a new countenance on his face, and a confident approach to life that causes people to see God and put their trust in Him.

God led Jackson to change, which drove him to God. The result was a desire to grow and pray and seek God.

What tough changes would God like to carry you through?
How has your journey strengthened your trust in God?
In what ways have your difficulties caused people to see God?

_____
_____
_____
_____

Trusting God on our journey encourages others to trust God in their journey.

WHY GOD IS WORTHY OF OUR TRUST

I have come to the place in my life where I know with certainty, dear God, that You alone are worthy of my trust. I don't have to figure it out. You already have! You have created a perfect plan for me, and I can trust You completely because You never fail. You always keep Your promises. My journey has taken me toward You, and I know without a doubt, I can trust You in every moment.

GUIDANCE FROM THE SOVEREIGN PLANNER

Before the mountains were brought forth, or ever you had formed the earth and the world, from everlasting to everlasting you are God.

PSALM 90:2

Clevelanders have the privilege of attending concerts performed by our Cleveland Orchestra. Attending a concert with my husband, Greg, I noticed the orchestra was divided into various sections of woodwinds, brass, percussion, strings, and keyboards. As the musicians were led by the conductor, I came to realize the compositions were a journey each musician had a part in, but not one of them played the complete piece. Each had only a part. The conductor oversaw the entire symphony, and the musicians had complete trust he would guide them to enter into the piece correctly when their instrument was called for. The conductor understood the end results and what was needed to get there to create a beautiful masterpiece that mesmerized the audience. The conductor saw the beginning to the end, the completion as all parts of the symphony came together. Not one musician tried to contradict the conductor's direction or take over his lead; they trusted him.

God oversees the entire symphony of creation. He understands the parts needed for each movement and how each movement interacts to form the ending masterpiece. The sovereignty of God explains His rule over creation. He is over all because He created all. God knows the end from the beginning and has orchestrated His plan from the beginning not only for creation but for each person He has created. God has a purpose or plan with respect to human affairs, but often we think we have our lives all figured out:

> For my thoughts are not your thoughts, neither are your ways my ways, declares the Lord. For as the heavens are higher than the earth, so are my ways higher than your ways and my thoughts than your thoughts. For as the rain and the snow come down from heaven and do not return there but water the earth, making it bring forth and sprout, giving seed to the sower and bread to the eater, so shall my word be that goes out from my mouth; it shall not return to me empty but it shall accomplish that which I purpose, and shall succeed in the thing for which I sent it. (Isaiah 55:8–11)

Rather than looking to God for help, we plan and do our best to determine the path for our lives. In some things we succeed, but in many ways we fail. We cannot control all the happenings that occur, and often we do not understand the part they play or how to move forward. We follow our own ways.

Often I look at my life like a puzzle. So many pieces are colorful and beautiful, yet some seem so dark to me. They seem to belong to another puzzle and do not make sense. I cannot see how they fit together, or if they ever will. I do not know what piece goes next. I cannot see the whole puzzle. But God does. He already knows the full picture. He sees the beautiful masterpiece and knows how all the pieces fit together.

Before time began, God knew each of us and created us to live in a certain way. He uses all the puzzle pieces in our lives and fits them together in the right way and at the right time. While the shape and the connections may not make sense to us, His ways and thoughts are not ours. He sees the masterpiece and fits the pieces together with that picture in mind.

When we surrender our plans to God's, we allow Him to join the pieces together to achieve the purpose for which He created us. Our holy and eternal God has a master plan for each of us with the end result being a beautiful, glorious masterpiece. As God oversees the entire symphony, He intertwines our purpose with that of others to create movements that bring good to us and glory to Him. All the movements of our lives lead to His ending symphony.

Trusting your sovereign God provides peace and joy, knowing you do not have to figure it all out. You just need to trust Him in the placement of the pieces, even when you cannot make sense of them. God truly knows you better than you know yourself. He created you for a specific purpose with His final masterpiece in mind.

How is God calling you to trust as He fits your puzzle pieces together?
What steps can you take to allow God to fulfill His created purpose for you?

_____

_____

_____

_____

Trust God to bring all the parts of your personal symphony to completion.

PROTECTION FROM THE CREATOR

*My help comes from the Lord,
who made heaven and earth.*

PSALM 121:2

Psalm 121 is a song of ascent. The children of Israel were headed toward Jerusalem to worship God. There is a movement out of captivity to a place of safety with the mountains surrounding them. The mountains are like a fortress around them as they head toward Jerusalem. As this journey is made, David recognizes the true source of his help:

> I will lift up my eyes to the hills. From where does my help come? My help comes from the Lord, who made heaven and earth. He will not let your foot be moved; he who keeps you will not slumber. Behold, he who keeps Israel will neither slumber nor sleep. The Lord is your keeper; the Lord is your shade on your right hand. The sun shall not strike you by day, nor the moon by night. The Lord will keep you from all evil; he will keep your life. The Lord will keep your going out and your coming in from this time forth and forevermore. (Psalm 121)

Because the mountains surrounded him like a fortress on the journey through them, David sensed the protection they offered. However, as he looked to the hills, he knew that his true protection came from the Maker of those hills.

Like He did for David, God surrounds us with His protection each and every day. He watches over each part of our life to keep us from evil. He sustains us through our journey. He guides and protects each step of the way.

I know this, yet I am also reminded that bad situations and struggles still take place in my life. In his walk through the mountains, David knew that though he was surrounded by God's protecting presence, there were still dangers lurking behind the rocks—wild animals, bandits, falling rocks or trees. As with David, there are dangers in our lives causing struggles and difficulties. In this, we also are surrounded by God's protection. He never sleeps or is weary. He is always right there watching us and keeping us like a father watching over his precious children. Nothing separates us from His perfect love.

When that realization fully hits, trusting God should be easy. We can trust Him because He is trustworthy. He is always there guiding and protecting us every single step of the way and will do so for each of us until He takes us to be with Him. However, experiences of life cause us to look at the dangers surrounding us rather than the God surrounding the dangers. He asks us to reach out our hand, cling to His hand already reaching out to us, and willingly allow Him to guide us along His journey. He never promised there would not be hard times and dangers along the path. He did promise that He would never leave us or forsake us. Asaph captured this in Psalm 73:

> Nevertheless, I am continually with you; you hold my right hand. You guide me with your counsel, and afterward you will receive me to glory. Whom have I in heaven but you? And there is nothing on earth that I desire besides you. My flesh and my heart may fail, but God is the strength of my heart and my portion forever. For behold, those who are far from you shall perish; you put an end to everyone who is unfaithful to you. But for me it is good to be near God; I have made the Lord God my refuge, that I may tell of all your works.
> (Psalm 73:23–28)

You will encounter both blessings and difficulties in life. God has promised to walk with you through both. He has promised He would be with you each step in your life journey. It is not enough to know who God is. You need to believe God is who He says He is and will do in your life what He has promised He will do. He has promised to never leave you. He will be your refuge and your strength. As you draw near to Him, He will draw near to you. Not only will His nearness cause an overwhelming security and growing trust, but your life will also be a testimony of the amazing refuge you have found in God.

What dangers are you looking at?
It is good to be near God. What is your plan to stay there?

_____

_____

_____

_____

The Maker of the mountains asks you to join His journey.
Will you reach for His hand today?

CERTAINTY IN HIS TRUSTWORTHINESS

God is not man, that he should lie, or a son of man, that he should change his mind. Has he said, and will he not do it? Or has he spoken, and will he not fulfill it?

NUMBERS 23:19

Excitement filled the air as people from all walks of life made their way to the docks in Southampton, England, on April 10, 1912. The British passenger liner *Titanic* was scheduled to depart for its maiden voyage. Upon entering the ship, first-class passengers began their climb on the sweeping curve of the Grand Staircase to their rooms. Third-class passengers looked beyond their lesser accommodations due to the excitement of a new beginning as the ship left port heading for New York City in the United States.

First class on the *Titanic* was the pinnacle of luxury and comfort, but even the lower classes enjoyed better accommodations than normal. The *Titanic* was built with advanced safety features, including watertight compartments and doors. It was considered unsinkable, as were most ships of that day.

On April 15, after the *Titanic* ran at full speed into an iceberg, promises of its unsinkability failed; within two hours and forty minutes of striking the iceberg, the ship sank. Not only did the ship fail its passengers with safe passage, an insufficient number of lifeboats were provided, which failed to transport all the passengers to rescue vessels, which also failed to arrive in time. Crew members failed passengers by not being trained properly for evacuation, and Captain Smith failed to take iceberg warnings seriously. So many things failed, resulting in the deaths of 1,517 souls.

So many things in life cannot be counted on. They fail, and even people we trust fail us. Only One can be trusted all the time, no matter what. Our God does not fail. Moses reminded the children of Israel of this as he transferred leadership to Joshua. "Be strong and courageous. Do not fear or be in dread of them, for it is the Lord your God who goes with you. He will not leave you or forsake you" (Deuteronomy 31:6).

God would not leave His people or fail them in any way regardless of the choices they would make. He promised to always be present with them and assist them. In fact, this was not just a promise for the Israelites, but for all believers. Throughout the entire Bible, God's promises are kept. All of His prophecies have been and will be accurately fulfilled. Even as the angel shared God's plan for Mary, he reminded her of our unfailing God as he said to her, "For no word from God will ever fail" (Luke 1:37 NIV). With God, nothing is impossible. What He says, He will bring about. What He has planned, He will do. That has been clearly seen throughout the pages of Scripture.

God also declares of Himself: "God is not man, that he should lie, or a son of man, that he should change his mind. Has he said, and will he not do it? Or has he spoken, and will he not fulfill it?" (Numbers 23:19).

Men change their minds and purposes due to changes in direction, unexpected happenings, wrong information, or emotions. They change their minds and break their word. They cannot be counted on. There is not a single person on this earth we can completely rely on because at some point, their word will fail—sometimes not through any fault of their own.

This is never the case with God. He never changes His mind or withdraws His promises. The Word of God is testimony to the infallibility of God's very words. He will never lie, and He will never fail. It is against His very nature, and because of that, He can be trusted above all else. We can always completely rely on Him, His Word, and His promises—always.

So what will you choose? Will you stay where you are in your unbelief, stay paralyzed where you are in your ways and your desires? Or you can decide to move forward in uncertainty but in the knowledge that God will not fail. His ways can be trusted, and He will not fail you.

What areas of life do you struggle to trust God with? What keeps you from trusting an unfailing God?

_____

_____

_____

_____

Surrendering to the Creator recognizes His sovereign control over the life He created us to live.

CONFIDENT IN THE GOODNESS OF GOD

And we know that for those who love God all things work together for good, for those who are called according to his purpose.

ROMANS 8:28

I was born in Tennessee to a mom and dad I will never have the privilege to meet. Because of circumstances I will never know, they thought it best to give me up for adoption. Six weeks after I was born, I became a part of the Williams family. My daughter, Bethany, was also adopted. She was born in China, and after three years of paperwork and appointments, we were finally able to make her a part of the Perelka family.

To say that Bethany and I had a rough relationship is an understatement. We did not like each other at all! I did all I could to prepare for her arrival. As she began her adjustments, I studied her and learned about her with the goal of helping her become acclimated to a new country, a new home, a new family. Bethany was charming but strong-willed, and she did not want anyone in charge of her, especially not me. Often our eyes glared with anger at each other. How often I would cry out to God, questioning His plan. I was so sure adopting a little Chinese girl was what He had called us to do. I regretted adopting her and wished we hadn't.

I expressed this to my son, Benjamin, one day, and he reminded me that God brought her into our home, and He had a plan. Paul reminds us in Romans:

> And we know that for those who love God all things work together for good, for those who are called according to his purpose. For those whom he foreknew he also predestined to be conformed to the image of his Son, in order that he might be the firstborn among many brothers. And those whom he predestined he also called, and those whom he called he also justified, and those whom he justified he also glorified. (8:28–30)

God does have a purpose for each one of His children. For most of my journey with Christ, I felt like I was missing something. I felt I had no purpose, no relationship with God—at least not a growing one. I did all the things a good Christian should do, but I did not know how to get closer to God. I always asked God, *How?* How could I have this growing relationship with God that I saw others had? In His goodness, God pursued me and broke me through a little girl.

Bethany loved books, and in an attempt for us to bond, we began a project to organize the church library. One day in our short ride to church, God burdened my heart with how I was treating Bethany. I realized I was responding to her as I had been treated much of my life. I criticized her and worked to change her to the way I thought she should be. I did not make her feel special or loved. She couldn't see God because I had not shown Him to her. She was growing up and becoming just like me, but this wasn't the person I wanted her to be.

There in the church parking lot that day, I reached for my girl with tears streaming down my face and apologized to her for how I had treated her. At that moment God changed my heart, and everything clicked. I began to pursue God through prayer and studying His Word. I learned about the love of God. No, I did not change overnight and neither did Bethany, but growth began, not only between us but also between me and my Father.

God began a relationship of love with each one of us before we were even thought of. He had a purpose and plan. He knew exactly what He wanted to accomplish in each of our lives and what the outcome would be. In salvation through our faith and repentance of sin, we stand clean before a holy God. We are adopted into His family and become joint heirs with Christ. The Holy Spirit begins His work of sanctification. The process of making us holy is good and filled with God's grace. Some parts of this process are difficult and do not feel good, but God walks through each step with us and uses all things to accomplish His purposes and make us more like His Son. The completion of the sanctification by the Holy Spirit will be when we are glorified as we make our home in heaven.

As I think of how Bethany and I started out on our journeys, all I can do is be thankful for God's goodness. There is no guarantee that either Bethany or I would have come to have a saving faith in the Lord Jesus apart from being taken from our birth parents and becoming a part of families who led us to God. In His goodness, God put Bethany in my life to show me how to have a relationship with God. He continues His goodness in our lives in so many ways, and each separate part may not seem good. We may not understand each part, but each part is working together for the good we will see when the masterpiece He has created each of us to be is completed.

What are specific moments in your journey causing change or growth?

As you think of your own faith journey, how have you seen the goodness of God?

_____

_____

_____

_____

God's gracious goodness takes us through life's journey to the highest good we could ever be.

HE IS GOD AND WE ARE NOT

And those who know your name put their trust in you, for you, O Lord, have not forsaken those who seek you.

PSALM 9:10

So, my question is, do you trust God? I mean really trust Him. Do you trust Him when sorrow upon sorrow is laid at your door? Do you trust Him when the unfairness of life continues with no possibility of change? Do you trust Him when everyone around you has a good life but nothing seems to go right for you? Do you trust Him when tragedy strikes? Do you trust Him when the hard life you live has no end?

You see, God never said we would know exactly what was coming. He never said life would be fair. He never said we would not face situations that seem impossible to overcome. He may call us to do tasks that seem insurmountable. We may never understand why we endure some of the difficulties of life and why they continue to come or do not end. God has not called us to understand, to live a life free from hardship, or to have certainty that whatever we face will end. What He did ask is for each of us to trust Him completely every moment of every day, and He promised He would be with us. He doesn't ask us to face anything alone. Not only that, throughout the Bible He shows us why He is worthy of our trust.

The Lord passed before him and proclaimed, "The Lord, the Lord, a God merciful and gracious, slow to anger, and abounding in steadfast love and faithfulness, keeping steadfast love for thousands, forgiving iniquity and transgression and sin." (Exodus 34:6–7)

It is the Lord who goes before you. He will be with you; he will not leave you or forsake you. Do not fear or be dismayed. (Deuteronomy 31:8)

O Lord, God of Israel, there is no God like you, in heaven above or on earth beneath, keeping covenant and showing steadfast love to your servants who walk before you with all their heart. (1 Kings 8:23)

The Lord is my strength and my shield; in him my heart trusts, and I am helped; my heart exults, and with my song I give thanks to him. The Lord is the strength of his people; he is the saving refuge of his anointed. Oh, save your people and bless your heritage! Be their shepherd and carry them forever. (Psalm 28:6–9)

If the Lord had not been my help, my soul would soon have lived in the land of silence. When I thought, "My foot slips," your steadfast love, O Lord, held me up. When the cares of my heart are many, your consolations cheer my soul. (Psalm 94:17–19)

Who is a God like you, pardoning iniquity and passing over transgression for the remnant of his inheritance? He

> does not retain his anger forever, because he delights in steadfast love. He will again have compassion on us; he will tread our iniquities underfoot. You will cast all our sins into the depths of the sea. (Micah 7:18–19)

> Do not be anxious about anything, but in everything by prayer and supplication with thanksgiving let your requests be made known to God. And the peace of God, which surpasses all understanding, will guard your hearts and your minds in Christ Jesus. (Philippians 4:6–7)

Our God is all these things. He faithfully gives us grace for each moment, causing us to hope but also trust.

> But this I call to mind, and therefore I have hope: The steadfast love of the Lord never ceases; his mercies never come to an end; they are new every morning; great is your faithfulness. "The Lord is my portion," says my soul, "therefore I will hope in him." The Lord is good to those who wait for him, to the soul who seeks him. It is good that one should wait quietly for the salvation of the Lord. (Lamentations 3:21–26)

Every single day God provides His mercy and the grace needed for everything we will have to face that day. As sinners, we deserve nothing but the punishment we have earned, but in His goodness and grace, God gives us what we don't deserve. But for the mercy of God, things could be much worse. Because of God's mercy, because of who God is, we can trust Him. There is no one we can trust like we can trust this amazing God. God chooses to love us and walk us through all things. If we cannot trust God, who could we trust?

The Bible clearly reveals God is faithful and displays His very nature. Because He is God, He cannot go against His nature. When all in our life seems like a failure, remember you are walking with a God who does not fail. He keeps His promises. He will walk us through the journey He knew we needed to take even before we were born so that we will end our lives as the beautiful masterpieces He intended us to be.

So, my last question to you is, Will you trust Him?
Do I trust Him? As I have walked through this journey of life, I have found there is no other choice but to trust Him. So yes, I trust Him.

_____

_____

_____

Trust God, not just for the end He has promised you.
Take Him through the journey you are now on
as He leads you to that end.

ORDER INFORMATION

REDEMPTION
PRESS

Additional copies of this book can be ordered
wherever Christian books are sold.

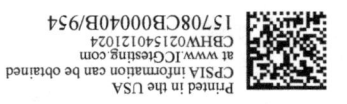